Praise for *Styling at the Top*

'I congratulate Shiva for his memoir *Styling at the Top* and hope Shiva's journey in life, his struggles and hard work will inspire the youth to become entrepreneurs and innovators.'

CH Vidyasagar Rao, Governor of Maharashtra

'The book is a poignant tale of Shiva's rise to becoming an acclaimed hairstylist from his humble beginnings. Of particular significance is the chapter on tutoring young stylists, a training initiative conceived under the MANAS (Maulana Azad National Academy for Skills) programme... The struggle Shiva experienced in this journey will surely motivate young hair stylists and will prove to be a guiding force for them to be successful in their career.'

Devendra Fadnavis, Chief Minister of Maharashtra

'*Styling at the Top* makes for compelling reading and gives a powerful message for the young generation. Shiva's remarkable life journey shows the path to achieve success is only through hard work and dedication. For one who had absolutely nothing to evolve into someone to reckon with—Shiva is a shining example.'

Uddhav Thackeray, Shiv Sena Chief

'I am delighted to read your book *Styling at the Top*. It brings to light that a youngster can create his own path in a chosen career and can also flourish in life. The book has been produced with useful information and motivation.'

Padma Vibhushan D Veerendra Heggade, Dharmadhikari, Shree Kshetra, Dharmasthala, Karnataka

'The book shows us the big picture of Shiva's life. It takes us on his life's journey, a tumultuous one, of hardships and difficult times; and then it illustrates how he has achieved success all on his own with his strength of mind and fortitude.'

Madhur Bhandarkar, National Award-winning filmmaker and Padma Shri awardee

'Shiva is a super achiever in the true sense of the word. His remarkable success story and outstanding contribution to the industry is inspirational for today's young generation who look out for role models. May he rise and shine further from strength to strength.'

Raveena Tandon, National Award-winning Actress

'Shiva is one of the most hardworking persons that I have come across. The way he has risen from scratch to becoming a brand is really commendable. His life is an inspiration for a lot of people and the book tells us all about this and how he has evolved as a creative hairstylist.'

Sonu Sood, Actor

Styling at the Top

The Journey of Shiva

Bollywood's Celebrated Hairstylist

JAYASHREE SHETTY

AMARYLLIS

AMARYLLIS
An imprint of Manjul Publishing House Pvt. Ltd.
•7/32, Ansari Road, Daryaganj, New Delhi 110 002
Website: www.manjulindia.com
Registered Office:
•10, Nishat Colony, Bhopal 462 003 – India

This edition first published in 2019

Cover design by Bhavi Mehta

ISBN 978-93-89143-09-6

Printed and bound in India by Thomson Press (India) Ltd.

CONTENTS

Praise for Shiva

At the core, Shiva is always keen to learn new things. He has a passion for hairdressing, hair designing and beauty. He has the ambition to excel in his field and is willing to put in a lot of hard work. These qualities constitute the pillars of a successful business.

Shiva can be best described as a people's person. He does not limit his knowledge and skill to himself; instead, he likes to take it forward through his staff and other people who are keen to learn from him and from Shiva's salons. He shares a passion for education and sharing information similar to the core values that we believe in at L'Oreal.

I wish Shiva and his team the very best. L'Oreal will always be with Shiva and his salons.

—Aseem Kaushik, Director,
L'Oreal Professional Products

AUTHOR'S NOTE

Think big, dream big,
and the results will be big.

—Anonymous

One would think that the story of a hairstylist, that too one based in the country's glamour hub, Mumbai, and working in the midst of film stars, movies and the fashion world, would be full of gossip, spiced with juicy titbits about tinsel town. Far from it.

This is the life story of hairstylist Shivarama Bhandary, or Shiva as he is popularly known. A heartrending tale of misery and grief, of a life led with dignity and grace, and marked by hard work. For readers, it exemplifies the fact that despite adversities, they can reach the pinnacle of their career if they set their goals right.

The above adage, holds true for Shiva, a self-made businessman. Starting from a poky shop in an industrial belt in north Mumbai, he goes on to own twenty salons, some exclusive parlours for women and signature salons in the upmarket areas of Walkeshwar and Juhu.

Shiva's—as also the man behind the brand—has come a long way. And, surely, is here to stay.

Shiva has ambitious plans laid out, with an impressive line of bespoke salons, new projects to expand in the beauty and hair segment, to groom fresh talent and to take the establishment forward.

Shiva has already launched his own line of beauty and hair care products under the sub-brand 'Shiva's Trends'. Mostly made with rare herbs and natural ingredients, they include shampoos, conditioners, skin serums, scrub gels, massage gels, massage creams, facial packs and skin toners. They are being used in his salons already and have received excellent feedback from customers. The products are suitably made for all skin types and are available for purchase.

This memoir is relevant for the sake of posterity—that is how Shiva explained it to me when he planned to chronicle his life.

His autobiographical memory took him way back to the time when he was a child, aged five, helping him pick out minute incidents like a visually rich pictorial representation from his past. To put together the innumerable events he was keen to share with readers, the book is filled with myriad anecdotes and episodes. The chapter-wise narrative depicts various stages of his life, all of them extraordinary.

Indeed, it was not a childhood made up of the usual memorable moments that children savour—good times spent with family and friends, at school, playing, studying… Shiva never did get to experience anything of the sort. You cannot even call it a childhood, for he had to grow up fast, quit school and start earning. But now, with his two school-going children, he seems to be reliving the part and enjoying it too.

Incidents from his life, even those with a tenuous connection to haircutting, therefore, had to be elaborated to understand what moulded him into becoming the strong-willed and determined person that he is.

Shiva's life spans two contrasting periods of time—his rural existence and his urban lifestyle.

It is a tale besieged with the endless woes of a farm boy in penury as his widowed mother struggled to make ends meet. The tragic circumstances forced him to work from morn to dusk as an unpaid worker in the fields and in a barber shop besides being subjected to caning every day by an alcoholic, cantankerous uncle. On many nights, he reminisces, he went to sleep hungry, weary and sore to his bones. Those were his most testing times.

Despite all the odds stacked against him, he trained in the art of hairstyling from one of the world's best academies and also worked overseas—an experience that eventually made him a top hairstylist, a favourite in Bollywood and a successful businessman.

The will to succeed and make sense of a chaotic and difficult life led him to take several life-altering decisions. This holds true even today, be it a personal situation or a business decision, he does not hesitate to evaluate conditions and then take a decisive stand. In fact, he appears to thrive on challenges.

Besides being a hairstylist, teacher and businessman, Shiva is also a philanthropist, offering his services to old-age homes, children's charities and religious organisations.

I first met Shiva to interview him on a quirky hairstyle he had designed on a client's hair in 2001. At that time a sting operation on an arms deal had rocked the nation. Shiva decided to use the logo of the media house responsible for the scoop as the design for his client's hair. This feat was covered by the Reuters news wire and appeared worldwide. Many friends and even clients from the Middle East connected with him instantly.

Then onwards, his designs, mostly related to the news of the day, about cricket and soccer matches, general elections, and portraits of film stars and even beauty pageants, were a rage. Queues outside his salons were proof that his talent was well appreciated and clients were keen to sport his wacky haircuts.

Taking time out of his busy schedule, Shiva shared details of those umpteen turning points and upheavals that shook him early in life and the consequent torture, ridicule and discrimination he had to suffer within his own family. Over many sessions, sipping lemon tea sans sugar and nibbling nutrition-packed biscuits—a result of turning health-conscious, now crucial to keeping up with the pace of work—he spoke candidly about those twists and turns.

A large part of the recording had him pouring out his thoughts with ease, vividly recalling incidents, saying that they were still fresh in his mind. There was never a feeble attempt at remembering any episode. He would even voice his thoughts in high decibels—these instances would more often than not come up whenever an anecdote struck his mind like a bolt of lightning.

But there were occasions when he could not hold back his grief and sorrow; recollecting painful memories from childhood or when Harinakshi, his first wife, was ailing and carrying on with unbearable pain while undergoing treatment for cancer. Now he stays with his mother, his wife Anushree and their two children in Mumbai.

To chronicle a memoir can turn out to be an agonising experience for the narrator, living those harrowing phases many times over. Others would describe the process as cathartic, in that it allows the narrator to share his angst and open up in an unbridled, free manner about all those moments that may not have been spoken of earlier, except perhaps with dear ones.

Grief turns in due course into a hard sediment and settles down in the depths of a burdened heart. At some stage in life, it requires a vent to purge, if not wholly, at least partially; to recollect those horrific details much against one's wishes, and then to forgive oneself and others.

Over time, Shiva does feel that he has emotionally toughened up and is therefore able to unwind in front of students who come to pursue beauty and hair courses at his academy. He believes that sharing experiences from his own life with the students would help set an example for the young minds. He hopes that they would be able to take all the obstacles that life throws at them in their stride.

Even so, his eyes do well up. His voice breaks with sadness. He would begin to rub his wet palms, then sip some water and resume talking. The fact that he would promptly keep aside those painful memories and smile again mirrors his determination to see through the worst and get on with work.

It depicts how much he is willing to overcome adversities, optimistically embrace the positives and focus on accomplishing his dreams. There are few people like him who would have withstood such harsh blows in life and emerged strong and sane. That truly is the mark of an achiever.

To write this memoir—apart from his own narrations and meeting people with whom he had interacted—visits were made to his hometown, to salons where he had worked before starting out on his own, as well as to the village places and Mumbai chawls where he had lived.

It was equally important to see him go about his daily work, his interactions with customers, his impressions of people and to observe his responses to them. It was imperative to be a viewer, to watch moments unfold and get a perspective of things without seeming to be an intrusion. To be out of the frame, so to speak, and get a proper picture composition.

The celebrations to mark Shiva's salon business completing twenty-five years made for a telling sight—the jubilee function was a runaway success, showcasing his entire body of work and portraying his talent. It was a significant period, marking the hairstylist's long-drawn opus coming to fruition. It also signalled a new phase for a coiffeur who has always wanted to excel and challenge himself further.

Guests were spilling out into the adjoining area where cocktails and dinner were being served, but the man at the helm was sitting alone on the steps of the podium that had just showcased a stunning hair fashion extravaganza. He looked a tad sad wiping the sweat off his brows. He seemed quite disconnected from his immediate surroundings, even the presence of his son Rohil who was playing nearby did not distract him.

It is never easy to soak in the joy of success after an excruciatingly long period of distress and sorrow. Happiness sometimes is an encumbrance.

It is, therefore, a privilege and an honour to write his memoir and I would like to thank Shiva for giving me this opportunity and, in a way, be instrumental in bringing his story to the world.

Dr Ghanshyam Bhimani, Mumbai's well-known psychiatrist and a long-time friend of my husband, Gopal Shetty, thank you very much, Doctor. You have suggested a wonderful and an appropriate title for the book—*Styling at the Top*. The word 'top' is short and sweet and fittingly conveys the crowning glory evident in Shiva's work—his ability to work magic on people's hair and him being the best in the field.

Gopal Shetty, a still and TV news photographer, thanks a lot for all your support and help. Without you, this book would not have been possible. Gopal's association with Shiva goes back to 1997, when he produced news features on the hairstylist's achievements for television that were aired on ETV News, NTV and Mid-Day TV/Zee TV. He took photographs of Shiva at all the places we visited during the writing of the book.

Lakshmi Krishnan, our editor, thank you from the bottom of my heart for all your suggestions and for editing the book. Our chats and meetings over the book will be much cherished, not to mention our conversations on entirely new topics. They were jovial too and lightened the course of discussions while working on such an intense book.

My sincere thanks to Amaryllis: An Imprint of Manjul Publishing House. I am indeed thankful to Mr Vikas Rakheja, MD of Manjul, Mr Manoj Kulkarni, Ms Rashmi Menon, and the entire team, who have been associated with this book in various capacities.

Jayashree Shetty
Writer-Journalist

FOREWORD

Genius is one percent inspiration and ninety-nine percent perspiration.

—Thomas Alva Edison, American inventor, who gave the world the electric light bulb

It was but a small dream

As a young boy, I had a simple wish. I fancied running a pint-sized barber shop made out of coconut branches in a village near Mangalore, in southern Karnataka. My requirements were limited: a cheap bamboo stool for the client to sit on, a comb and a pair of scissors. A minuscule place would have been enough for me to make a modest sum, to look after my mother and our household.

More than four decades later, God has blessed me abundantly. I now have my own chain of salons, named 'Shiva's', running successfully in India's glamour capital, Mumbai. I have a wonderful family—a supportive mother, an encouraging wife and two adorable children who always make me smile—trustworthy friends I can count on, a host of well-wishers constantly guiding me, dedicated staff, and above all, a firmly loyal clientele who enjoy visiting my salons.

As I look back on my journey so far, my heart fills with gratitude for all the people who had faith in me and stood resolutely by my side, even during my darkest hours. I am fortunate to have them in my life.

Often those well-wishers asked me—*Shiva, why don't you write your life story?* And occasionally, I did mull over their suggestion. For it is true that my life has been an eventful journey, replete with extraordinary experiences of loss, pain, grief and victimisation. Of numerous challenges and setbacks that rendered me distraught and left me an emotional wreck. But resilience and hope always kept me upbeat.

People often ask me the secret behind my cheerfulness and fiercely optimistic outlook. They are curious to know what keeps me on my toes, what pushes me to explore exciting new ideas, notably in my profession as a hairstylist.

The need to share life stories is deeply human. The survivor instinct runs strong in our veins. The more life throws at us, the tougher we get. And we feel a compelling need to share our life experiences with others. I felt it too. So one day, I decided to share my story with the world. To tell it all like it happened, with the humble hope that I may motivate others fighting their own battles to keep their spirits strong and emerge triumphant.

✂

The early years of my life were spent in utter penury. Throughout my childhood and adolescence, and for a few years as an adult too, I have lived in abject poverty. My life was a constant struggle to overcome hardships, to wade through murky situations and walk successfully out of the muck. Instances of slights and insults, abuses and losses, were far too many. But if you have never had your hands dirtied, how will you ever learn to wash them clean? So my determination to succeed and aim higher kept me going through the ebb and flow. For I do firmly believe, no matter how dark the tunnel, a faint flicker of light is always there to help you get to the other, brighter side.

A tough, traumatic early life makes one grow wiser and more perceptive. When youngsters visit my salon today, I can't help noticing that something is amiss. Many young adults and new entrants to the beauty and haircare industry either flaunt a devil-may-care attitude or act startlingly reckless with their time and money. Their conduct towards their family and other social obligations leaves much to be desired; they need to be more responsible.

Spanning a career of more than forty years, a good chunk of which was given to building a brand name, I have met enough people to understand where these youngsters go wrong. I have seen pampered children squandering their pocket money. I have witnessed young men and women in a tearing hurry to acquire luxuries, without making any effort to earn money sincerely. Their hunger for worldly riches and the peer pressure to possess material comforts leads them to the wrong path. My message to this generation would be to be mindful of their actions, to value more the relationships and natural gifts they have been bestowed with, and to count their blessings.

I come from a humble background. My poor and uneducated parents lived in a village called Attur bordering the temple town Karkala, close to Mangalore. Nature dealt us her first blow when I was all of three—my father Krishna Bhandary passed away, leaving my mother Gulabi Bhandary, sister Shobha and me in the throes of poverty. My widowed mother struggled to make ends meet by stitching clothes. I had to drop out of school to help run our home. Soon after came another blow—I lost Shobha, who was just four years old, to starvation and lack of medical care.

Over the next few years, we moved from one uncle's house to another, hoping against hope for some relief. But every time, we were shown the door. My mother and I were homeless and penniless, and times were really hard. And yet, what mattered was that we were there for each other through thick and thin.

In India, villages still have large families made up of grandparents, uncles, aunts, and close and distant cousins. Tradition rules the roost, and in any matter, the decision is always taken by the eldest family member. The others simply follow suit; nobody questions the decision-maker, period.

When my father died, my uncles (guardians at different stages of my childhood) decided for me, and I simply obeyed their orders. It did not matter that these resolutions were of no benefit to my present or future; my services were merrily used to their advantage. Without a father to protect you, you become nobody's child; you are used as free labour.

On my paternal uncle's insistence, I joined his barber shop located in the tea gardens of Yelemadalu in Chikamagalur, a district bordering Mangalore. He took me in as an assistant and treated me like a servant, never passing up a chance to remind me that he was providing me with shelter and food for free. Paying me for my services was not even considered.

My days were spent watching my uncle give haircuts to customers. I tried to acquaint myself with a barber's paraphernalia by shaving my legs and arms, and using his scissors to cut my own hair. Once I became familiar with these devices, working on customers became an effortless task.

My alcoholic uncle unleashed his frustrations by beating and physically abusing his wife and me. The alcohol addiction became his nemesis. Slowly, he refused to attend to clients and assigned the work to me instead.

Working in Yelemadalu was a toxic combination of drudgery and frosty weather. To date, I detest cold climes. I am rather uncomfortable with the cold air that blows out of an air-conditioner even in Mumbai's hot and humid climate. I prefer a whirring fan any day to clean out the stale air in a room.

But all said, I do feel grateful that in a nondescript village, braving the bitter cold and living on subsistence, slaving away in that shop, I found my calling in life.

This profession has helped me win the hearts of many people, people whom I value and have the greatest respect for. I carry within me a spontaneous, deep feeling of commitment to serving clients. Even before clients express their choice of a haircut, I intuitively sense what they are looking for.

Being deprived of a formal school education inculcated in me a deeper understanding of the fact that every moment in life is invaluable. I feel time wasted is gone forever. To be a good listener, to pay heed to what people say is fundamental to my being. Each one of them, every person I interact with, I regard as a teacher.

I often advise my staff to snap out of their complacency, to think big and rise high. I would like to see them set aside some of their earnings for a rainy day and resist wasteful expenditure. My business ideology has been simple: save and grow. That is how I went from a small salon to establishing a chain of outlets. And that's how I hope to continue opening as many salons as I possibly can.

Way back in 1988, I set up a tiny shop named 'Shiva's Stylo' near the famous Wagle Estate, a place known to house small industries in Thane, a township outside Mumbai. This undistinguished place suited the budget I could afford from my small savings, and I had the advantage of owning the sole barber shop in the neighbourhood. Soon, industrial workers started trickling in, given the convenience factor. Later, school children also began to come in for their haircuts.

Though I was confident of my work, I was anxious about running a new venture. I had taken a risk by starting out on my own. If I failed, I could only blame myself. That was the only redeeming factor about this move. The first day I worked until 11 p.m., earning ₹165 for the entire day. It was a tidy little sum, and it also indicated that people had noticed my shop.

For the next fifty-five days, I worked continuously, without a weekly break, staying in the salon and sleeping on a narrow bench at night. The bench was not long enough to accommodate my legs, but my tired bones needed rest at the end of a hard day. The front door was kept ajar for the breeze to blow into the humid place, even though there was a big drain giving off a continuous stench right outside the doorstep.

Every day, I woke up at 5.30 a.m., made tea and boiled eggs for breakfast, on a stove set up in a corner of the shop. I bathed in the backyard at a municipal water tap and washed my clothes and the towels used on clients. I opened the shop at 7 a.m. sharp. Morning walkers were regular clients, followed by school children, and then industry workers came as time permitted, until late in the night. Workers hailing from South India, conversant in Kannada, Tamil and Malayalam (languages I was familiar with) became loyal customers. As the flow of clients picked up, taking lunch breaks became difficult. I survived on a staple of vada pav (bread bun stuffed with a fried dumpling made of spicy potato and garnished with chillies and garlic chutney) bought from a vendor's cart.

Over the next couple of months, more customers began to come in, so I hired a young apprentice to assist me. When the numbers swelled further, I hired three more boys, all from towns and villages near Mangalore. I still have a fairly large staff coming from the region that was formerly known as South Canara and is now divided between the Dakshina Kannada and Udupi districts. People who hail from this region, I feel, are quick learners with an abundant zeal for knowledge. They also encourage relatives and friends from back home to join them in their work, share meals and even their homes in Mumbai until they feel the need to settle down and raise a family. Many such village boys have stayed with me in my Thane apartment, where my mother cooked for everyone. A large number of my staff still stays there.

The Thane shop, now renamed 'Shiva's', is our flagship hair-salon. Started with second-hand furniture, including two well-worn chairs, a mirror panel and a used hairspray bottle, today it is a large, well-equipped area, providing a range of facilities for facial, manicure and pedicure treatments. Earlier, we used to get clients from the industrial belt and a few from residential areas; today, many old clients still come to us even as new ones from urban areas have grown in number.

The salon in Mulund was opened in 1993. Around this time, I met Harinakshi, my wife, who later passed away. She opened another parlour alongside, exclusively for women. This parlour, now refurbished, has a loyal clientele that has been visiting since the time Harinakshi was around. Shiva's then expanded to open a salon in Lokhandwala, Andheri, primarily to make a foray into the western suburbs where film and television clientele was a big draw. We started offering trendy hairdos, high-end beauty therapies and spa treatments. My connection with tinsel town was established when well-known and budding filmmakers as well as actors started visiting us for haircuts and beauty care. To further grow the chain, we added an outlet in Juhu. Simultaneously, Shiva's Training Academy at Andheri's Link Road started. The academy runs to a full schedule, with classes organised in a joint initiative with the Central Ministry of Minority Affairs' MANAS (Maulana Azad National Academy for Skills) and MT Educare, to train minority students in hair and beauty care, and enable them to set up their own businesses.

Other outlets followed at Malad, Girgaum Chowpatty near Marine Lines, Matunga, Bandra-Kurla Complex, Walkeshwar, the northern suburb of Dombivali with a special salon for women and an outlet in Moodbidri, a prominent educational centre near Mangalore. Anushree, whom I married after Harinakshi passed away, now assists me in administering the Lokhandwala and Juhu outlets. Given our vast client base and the large number of staff, both salons—one unisex and the other catering exclusively to women—need our undivided attention.

The bespoke Shiva's Signature Salon at the tony Malabar Hill, with its state-of-the-art facilities housed in a sprawling space, offers an exclusive range of services in keeping with the latest trends in the beauty industry. Our future plans include opening more such swish outlets and upgrading some of the older parlours to make them fit into the Shiva's Signature category.

Shiva's shares a strong bond with clients who have been visiting our salons for over thirty years since its inception in 1988. People who visited us as school boys have now grown into young men and some have become successful businessmen. A few have even started balding, but they remain loyal to Shiva's! Customers have moved residences, yet they look out for our nearest outlet. Someday I hope to see a Shiva's outlet in every city, town and village in India. That is my dream.

This book is the story of a wonderful journey; of how the brand Shiva's evolved into a name to reckon with. The founding of the brand runs parallel to the events that shaped my life, both personally and professionally. This book is also an effort to share some of those life-changing moments and anecdotes with readers. The contents are based on my narration in Kannada interspersed with Tulu, Hindi and a bit of English. I hope readers will feel my experiences and perhaps draw inspiration. If nothing else, let us together sail along the tidal ups and downs of a coiffeur's voyage.

Shivarama Bhandary
Hairstylist, Mumbai

A journey of a thousand miles
begins with one step.

—Lao Tzu, Chinese philosopher

chapter one

WIDOW'S PEAK

My First Job: Shaving a Widow's Head at the Tender Age of Twelve

Memories of that bleak morning are as fresh in my mind as the first dew of dawn. I faced my first professional assignment—to shave the head of a young widow. My paternal uncle, under whom I was training in a conventional way, so to speak, by simply watching and learning while he worked, had delegated this work to me. Perhaps he imagined I could manage the task easily, as it did not demand cutting hair in any particular way or giving it some shape. The fact was, I was still grasping the basics of haircutting.

I took up the task without hesitation. But the night before my first assignment, as I lay on the floor mat trying to sleep, I did wonder how to tackle it on my own. I reckoned what I had to do would be similar to shaving and trimming the beards of male clients. The same straight razor that smoothened out hair follicles from the jaw, chin and neck would work well on the head too. The hard scalp would be less of a challenge, I contemplated, since I had had enough experience handling sensitive skin. Besides, by then, I had mastered the art of running the blade deftly and smoothly, so as to not nick the skin.

Early next morning, I set off from home in the darkness, wrapping my tools—a straight razor and a comb—in a cloth tucked under my arm. I walked barefoot all the way, from the village where I stayed, Yelemadalu, to a distant village, Netragunda, where the Brahmin family lived.

I had to trek nearly four miles, crossing long stretches of tea and coffee estates, jumping over fences, and sliding under barbed wire barriers to successfully navigate the hilly terrain in the interiors of Chikamagalur. It was still dark and chilly, and not a soul was in sight. I could hardly see the mud path sheathed with twigs from coffee trees and stones scattered everywhere. I feared nothing. I was quite used to running in knickerbockers on unlit trails, combating insects that would leave me with bites on my spindly bare legs. A half-sleeved cotton shirt gave sufficient warmth and cover to the upper body.

The soft rustle of leaves whispering in the wind was somewhat soothing. The only other sound was my own breath, occasionally coming in a heaving huff while negotiating narrow paths.

I took a breather after descending to a plateau at the end of the coffee plantations. There were large swathes of paddy fields lying bare after a harvest. The rays of the rising sun had begun to sneak in through the thick foliage of tall coniferous and rubber trees, sparkling like stars on the shimmery surface of ponds and rivulets gently flowing by the countryside.

From a distance, as I approached the house, I could see the massive tile-roofed bungalow in the midst of the pasture. I took the path to the backyard, passing a cowshed. Near the well, I squatted on my haunches, rested my tool-wrap beside me, and began waiting for the first client of my life.

A deathly silence pervaded. A tree branch that snapped created quite a rattle, startling me. *Isn't there anyone in the house,* I wondered, trying to peep inside. The house was in mourning, I knew, but the obvious absence of other family members gave the place a ghostly feel. Even the cattle lay motionless. Far in the fields, I could hear a wild fox howling.

Shortly, a lady in a pristine white saree walked out and crouched on a wooden plank on the ground. She bowed her head low before me, but I could hear muffled sobs under her breath. I felt a sense of intimidation before running the blade. I was hesitant to snip off all her locks. An eerie silence engulfed the place. Feeling out of sorts, I simply asked her if I should cut her hair short.

What kind of a question was that, I wondered, immediately feeling silly. I had come to shave her head on my uncle's instructions. I think I was trying to reason out my own confusion—why would a woman want to tonsure her head? Obviously, she must have been forced to, much against her wishes.

I understood that it was a tradition she was being compelled to follow. I waited for her to say something. She lifted her head to speak, and then… How can I ever forget that look on her face—distraught, eyes vacant and hollow. She is a brave woman, I remember thinking.

It was the first time I was going to use the barber's straight razor, the absolute first time I was going to shave the head of a girl widowed in her twenties, and the first time I was about to work like that on the mane of a client.

In the briefest of words, she directed me to shave her head entirely. Thick ringlets of long, lustrous hair came cascading down her shoulders, falling on the cobbled backyard. To me they seemed to fall rather helplessly, hopelessly, on the ground of an ancient bungalow standing desolate in the midst of mountain ranges.

I was a little over twelve years of age, but like a true professional, I held my hand firm and steady to wield the tool with utmost precision. I ran the rudimentary blade from her forehead down to the nape, shaving strip after strip of long hair that had, until that moment, been flowing down quite strikingly to her waist.

In that moment of sadness, her petite frame seemed as tough as a rock. She was gathering the courage to face an eventuality. It was quite an ordeal for me, but I took this task set out for me as my duty. No matter how apprehensive I felt, I had to continue shearing her locks matter-of-factly. Within minutes, her head was shaven bald!

I remember wondering then about what life had in store for her, as I had heard village folk gossiping about the perils of a widowed life. In a priestly family of orthodox Brahmins, a community ranking high in India's complex caste hierarchy, the passing away of a husband would mean abiding by an old, rigid order. The young lady would live in isolation, secluded from all worldly trappings and all that may be interpreted to make up a good life. She would also become a social outcast.

Superstitious beliefs regarding widows ran rife. Some believed that widowhood was a form of penance for sins committed in one's previous life. The woman had to atone in the present life to be free of all wrongdoings that she may have committed in an earlier birth. Henceforth, her presence at a public event would be considered a bad omen. Her participation in religious ceremonies would be deemed unacceptable.

In a way, our society too is victim to this bigoted system, blindly following a barbaric practice. It fills me with sorrow to think that such a ritual has always prevailed, even though it is perhaps practised to a lesser extent these days. With changing times, the custom has become less harsh on young widows in the region I hail from, but there is still a long way to go before widows are seen as a part of mainstream society.

The young widow (I did not know her name) looked at

the heap of glossy black hair that had fallen around her feet and sobbed incessantly. It was a sign of things to come, of a doomed future.

On an emotional level, I felt the pain, but physically speaking, I was as limp and powerless as the scattered clumps of hair on the ground. I did not know what to say. I gathered courage and offered words of consolation. 'God is there. He will protect you,' I managed.

But I felt sad at her miserable state. She had lost her lovely long hair. I felt responsible in a rather indirect manner for depriving her of an essential feature of a woman's beauty. Why did it have to be me? Why did I have to be the one to shave her head?

A barber or a coiffeur does have a sense of responsibility towards the client. As hairdressers, we have an obligation to dress hair up, keep it in order, offer eye-catching styles, lend character to an ordinary mop and enhance a client's persona. Most of all, we want to see our clients walking out of our salons feeling happy with a new haircut. The one thing we would never like to do is to make someone look unattractive!

My first task then was no less than a contradiction—I had been required to make a woman look ugly! It is not for nothing that a woman's hair is considered her crowning glory, but here I was, depriving a woman of her most natural adornment—her flowing tresses. It broke my heart.

After the ritualistic shave, a traditional cleansing process followed. She had to bathe with cold water drawn by her from the well in the backyard and then enter the house. Life would never be the same. She would spend a lonely life, perhaps pursue some spiritual practice and attend to children.

From her mourning, ironically, I learnt something. It instilled in me a sense of courage as I compared our lives. She was a woman trapped in a traditional setup. Opportunities to make life worth living were few, if any. She was alone and helpless with a grim future staring her in the face.

They say there is a reason for everything that happens in life. I, who had always imagined myself as one of the most ill-fated beings around, now saw some hope. I felt that I was a young boy with many years ahead of me. I was cast out there in the open world. Perhaps I was not free just yet to do what I pleased under the autocratic shadow of my uncle, but, unlike the widow, at least I was not bound by shackles of the social kind. A hint of optimism was kindled in my heart.

Given an opportunity, I could fly as high as I aimed. I felt less unfortunate. And I felt brave—brave enough to cope with any adversities I might have to face in future.

I learnt a lot from my first client. I am indeed grateful and thankful to her. In my quiet moments, I silently say a prayer for her.

I completed my work in twenty minutes, after which a family elder offered me a cup of warm filter coffee. Gulping the brew, I packed my wrap of tools to return home on the same rugged path, now sunnier. I jumped over tiny boulders, ran down the crisscross path, evaded thorny bushes and took big strides to reach home. I had my next errand waiting.

I had never envisioned that haircutting would be my calling in life. That someday I would become a coiffeur, dress people's hair in attractive styles and be instrumental in transforming a client's personality, sometimes just by trimming a few strands.

Tonsuring as a matter of fact was practised, and still is, in some villages, as punitive action for crimes committed. Therefore, tonsuring has adverse connotations in matters of speech, like laying bets over an issue in which the loser shaves his head bald, or uses the phrase as an abuse to prove his opponent wrong. But the biggest religious significance of the custom bears out at the renowned Tirupati temple in Andhra

Pradesh, where devout men and women seek blessings and favours in lieu of their own hair. Looking back, I feel that I took to the task with an abiding sense of duty. I recollect holding the straight razor with complete confidence. The young woman had some boils on the head, perhaps as a result of an unwashed scalp. To avoid hurting her, I had used the scissors very cautiously around the blisters and sore areas.

I recollect the V-shape that formed above her forehead, a 'widow's peak' in coiffeur's parlance. It was distinctly obvious on her bare head. The widow's peak, steeped in myth and tradition across cultures, is now a universal style statement. I learnt the expression later in my career as a hairstylist. Some countries still believe the V-shape to be an inauspicious mark, while some avant-garde style icons go to great lengths to flaunt the widow's peak.

Apprenticing under my uncle, I took up similar tasks a few more times, visiting households in mourning as well as those revelling in celebratory functions. I had to shave the heads of sons after the passing away of fathers, or that of young boys during the coming-of-age ceremonies held in Brahmin families. Uncle could never wake up before sunrise to head to mourning households to perform the rite of shearing a widow's hair.

After leaving home in my quest for ambitious opportunities in the big world of hairstyling, I have mercifully never been in such tricky situations.

We learn something from everyone who passes through our lives... Some lessons are painful, some are painless, but all are priceless.

—*Unknown*

chapter two

DUTIFUL SON TRIUMPHS OVER EVIL

The Midwife Prophesies

The umbilical cord was wrapped around me like a sash from shoulder to waist, similar to the sacred thread worn by Hindu men during the coming-of-age ceremony.

The midwife prophesied it was a good omen. The elderly woman assisting in my birth at my ancestral home proclaimed that I would fight against all odds to become successful in whatever I chose to do in life. She foretold a celebrated future and conveyed her forecast to my mother, aunt and elders in the family, saying the newborn baby was a blessed boy.

I was born on 23 April 1962, according to my paternal uncle Govinda Bhandary, who showed me an entry he had apparently made in his diary on the day of my birth. I observe my birthday on the same day because my uncle meticulously maintained a book in which he would make notes about all money matters and transactions that took place in his home or salon (the place where I apprenticed). Ahead in the story, I record further details of my stay with him.

As per custom, my mother had to deliver her first-born at her parents' home. Since both her parents had passed away, she delivered at her stepsister Kamala Bhandary's house. My birthplace, therefore, is a tiny hamlet called Nagoli near Attur, Karkala, where I spent my early childhood.

Today, my aunt's son Sunder Bhandary stays here in a newly built structure. The thatched house where I was born is now a new cement structure given out on lease. The well in the compound, my mother tells me, was a place she was wary of, because I would waddle towards the wall to peep in. She was constantly afraid I might fall into the deep hole that was the only source of water for the family. I think I wandered towards it because I often saw my mother drawing water from the well.

In the same village is a venerated Venugopal temple. As is the custom, my mother approached the priest there to have my horoscope cast so that he could recommend auspicious letters of the alphabet that matched my birth stars for me to be given a suitable name. The priest advised my mother that my name should begin with the letters '*Sha*' or '*Ra*', and he suggested the names of two powerful Hindu gods—Shiva and Rama. Shiva is the destroyer of evil in the Hindu holy trinity and Rama is the dutiful king from the epic *Ramayana*. Mother decided it had to be a combination of both names—Shivarama. When I was young, she fondly called me Anna, meaning elder brother, a common, reverential form of address for men or boys in Karnataka. Children are affectionately called Anna.

Mother now calls me Shivarama, while I am just Shiva for everyone else. My business and the line of salons go by the name Shiva's.

Quitting School to Help Mother

My mother had six siblings in all, including a brother and a sister, and stepbrothers and stepsisters. After my father's death, my mother and I kept hopping from one house to another, living with relatives who very grudgingly offered us shelter.

Anand Bhandary, Mother's stepbrother, took us to his ancestral home located amidst long stretches of fields at Kabettu village, near Karkala. A farmer with a large family of as many as thirty members, my uncle was caretaker to his sons, daughters and their families, including a grandmother and a few babies, all staying under the same roof. Strangely, none of the male members stepped out to work; everyone preferred to live off the farm produce.

At all times, it was a house packed with people, but nobody cared for my mother and me, nobody spoke kind words—as one would normally expect—to a kin in distress. We were seen like an added burden to an already burgeoning family. When meals were ready, I would see the elders rushing into the kitchen and feeding their children. We would hesitate to join them, and nobody would invite us either. The clanging of pots, pans and serving plates during lunch hour would stir my hunger. After everyone had finished with their meals, my mother, sister and I would hesitantly enter the kitchen to find huge empty pots on the mud oven. We would just about manage to scrape off some leftover rice broth and grains floating at the bottom of the vessel. We never had adequate food.

My mother figured out that the family members were not in favour of us staying here. Quarrels and misunderstandings erupted frequently and began to get worse day after day. One day, following a bitter exchange of words, we were shown the door.

Mother's brother Sanjeev Bhandary lived in nearby Attur, so we moved to his house. Here my mother tried to take up a tailoring job to contribute to household expenses while I attended St. Lawrence, a Kannada-medium school. What I cherish most about school is the time I had to recite a couplet in the native Tulu language for a school event. Donning a false moustache and big headgear, I recited the following three lines:

Yaan ori Bambayga poodu varsha pathande (I have completed a decade in Bombay)

Yenka ette oorugu poodu madme aapodu (Now I want to go to the village to get married)

Yanna kaitta notu ondu savira katande (I hold in my hands notes counting ten hundreds)

(The couplet above is a popular rhyme recited in villages near Mangalore, and holds true for people who have moved out to settle in Mumbai. I too left the village to work in Mumbai, established myself, and then went back to the village to marry a girl from our milieu.)

Midway through my recitation, my eyes fell on a sea of people in the auditorium. I developed stage fright and ran away from the podium. This fear of speaking in front of an audience plagues me even today! I still feel nervous when I'm invited to speak at functions where I'm required to stand on stage and address a crowd to share my success story. But I am making an effort and slowly beginning to overcome the phobia.

In 2012, St. Lawrence School held a special function to honour me. The school authorities said they felt extremely proud to have me, a successful entrepreneur in the salon business, among their alumni. The principal, Father Arthur Pereira, told his students that I was a role model, a fine example for them, and he talked about how hard I had worked to earn a good name. It is humbling to be part of a school that acknowledges my work and recognises me as an alumnus, even though I only studied up to Class Five. I had to drop out after that because of financial compulsions at home. Every time I visit my alma mater, I pay a visit to the revered St. Lawrence Church in the neighbouring school compound. I have spent many difficult hours praying there.

Education is like a pillar of strength in one's life, and there is never any substitute for it. I learnt the hard way in my formative years that lack of education is a hindrance to one's smooth progress. I lacked the guidance of teachers and instructors in my life. But over time I began to understand that learning is a continuous process. Which is why, to me, education is about learning from my day-to-day interactions with people. A keen observer, I try to watch the world around me, listen carefully, imbibe and then think over how well I can apply what I have learnt when faced with a particular situation. This process is what I consider my schooling. It has been like this all my life.

We stayed at Sanjeev uncle's house for two years. During this time, owing to severe ill health, my sister passed away. That fateful night, I was staying at my cousin Krishna's house and I was not even told about the tragedy. Perhaps the family thought I was too young to be told about her death. My mother later told me that my sister called out my name in her last moments. While I was drifting off to sleep that night, I overheard Krishna's father inform the family about her passing away. My mother was devastated, having seen her child die in front of her eyes. To me, not having her around was the saddest part; I felt a vacuum that could never be filled by another. '*Anna, Anna...*' that is how she called out to me usually, and those were the only words she uttered as she left this world. This wasn't my first encounter with losing a loved one, but when my father had died I was too small to understand the gravity of the situation.

Staying at Sanjeev uncle's house was not easy either. Family members began objecting to our presence, and it was soon painfully clear that they were waiting for us to move out. Differences had arisen among family members right from the beginning and discrimination was evident in the behaviour and treatment meted out to us. If I went to get a haircut at my uncle's salon, my hair would be pulled and tugged, with a few knocks landing on my head. I would be rebuked and asked to go to a roadside barber since I 'did not deserve' the services of a posh salon with faux leather-covered chairs and fancy mirrors. I had no money, so I realised the only option was to try chopping my hair on my own with the scissors available at home.

For a single woman with a really young son, the situation was hard on my mother. She helped with household chores, yet there was constant bickering and squabbling, resulting in clashes between Uncle's wife Janaki and my mother. One day, a particularly vocal exchange ended in a slew of profanities. We were promptly ordered to leave the house as Janaki threw our belongings along with some utensils out of the house. Once again, we were homeless.

Mother and I stayed out in the open for three days, cooking food under a coconut tree in the compound. We were just the two of us in this hour of crisis, penniless and with no roof above our heads.

We set up some stones to make an oven and lit a fire in it with twigs collected from the compound. We placed a vessel over it and cooked our meals. On the third day, the rice broth tasted like soap water. Someone had played a cruel prank to drive us out of the compound. Fights erupted again as family members began abusing us and driving us out of the premises. Those were tough times. One set of troubles followed another. My mother was inconsolable. I had never seen her so helpless in all my life. What could a lone woman with a child do?

As they say, when all doors close, a faint light flickers in the dark. That glint of light came in the form of Kariminabai, a lady in the neighbourhood, who gave us shelter, allowing us to rent an adjoining part of her house for a paltry sum. The leased place came with additional chores for me—watering the garden, plucking fruits and coconuts, and other sundry work that she required. I decided to quit school in the fifth grade to supplement my earnings towards running our house and paying rent. Mother continued to work at the tailoring unit. For extra income, she took individual orders to sew clothes at home. I can vividly recall her sitting hunched over, sewing skirts and blouses on a second-hand machine for the village people.

It took us a while to settle down at Kariminabai's house. I discovered that when one is helpless and penniless, the chances of people pointing fingers at the slightest provocation are far greater. Kariminabai had two daughters—Jessie, the older one, who was studying in the eleventh, and Benny, the younger one, in the tenth grade. Benny lost her pen one day and pointed a finger at me for stealing her prized possession.

Kariminabai promptly yelled at my mother for my alleged transgression. Upset at receiving complaints, my mother refused to hear me out when I pleaded that I was innocent. She caned me to make me confess that I had indeed taken the pen and that it ought to be returned to the rightful owner. My back was covered in long welts from the stick and I was in terrible pain. But I remained resolute; why should I plead guilty when I had not taken the pen?

Eventually my mother understood that I was speaking the truth. Overcome with grief, she wept and rubbed oil on my back to relieve the pain. She felt sorry for beating me so badly and felt worse for believing such false allegations. It was unfortunate that Mother was always at the receiving end, given her vulnerable position in society; her troubles were never-ending.

In due course, Kariminabai's house turned out to be a reasonably better place to stay—we lived there for over four years. She was happy that I meekly followed all her orders without complaining. My work included drawing water from the well, watering plants, plucking jasmine and hibiscus flowers, cultivating vegetables like gourds, red amaranth and her favourite creeper, *basale soppu* (Malabar spinach). I had to dig long bamboo poles into the ground and tether them to horizontal ones so that the thick green stems curled and rested along the trellis for sufficient support. I tended chikkoo (sapota), guava, mango and jackfruit trees, looked out for ripened fruits and drove out the insects.

Kariminabai, a single mother fending for her two daughters, was an unabashed taskmaster. She would make me brazenly carry one mudi—a bundle made of hay and rope in which rice grains are tightly packed; one of these bundles contained nearly thirty-eight kilograms of rice—on my head, all the way from the Attur bus stand to the house. This was the yearly stock of rice she would buy, travelling in a bus from a nearby farm. I would be told to wait at the stand to carry the heavy load as it was impossible for her to lug it around, and she refused to hire help because she would have had to pay. My legs would waddle and swing back and forth as I tried to clutch the bundle upright on my head while walking the nearly half-a-kilometre stretch home. Panting for breath and my body soaked in perspiration, barefoot in the blistering heat, I would obediently follow her.

One day, I had to go to the market to buy the newspaper, for it carried the Class Ten board exam results. Benny was eagerly waiting for her results. As usual, I washed up the only pair of short pants I had and spread them out to dry near the fireplace, where boiled brown rice and sambar (a spicy lentil soup) were being cooked for lunch. Usually, while the pair of knickerbockers dried, I would wrap a towel around my waist and continue with work.

That day, though, I smelt burning fumes. I looked around and was shocked to see my shorts on fire. I rushed to blow out the fire and dust away black soot, only to find a gaping hole in the khaki pair. I peeped into the singed gap, it was rather big and unfit to wear. I was in a fix. How could I wear torn clothes? I thought of mending it. Mother was not at home to help.

I had seen her sew many times. I tore out a piece from an old, ragged cloth umbrella to stitch up the patch, not realising that I had sewn the patch onto the outside of the shorts, instead of inside. The haphazard patchwork, which would have made a trendy statement today, looked like a tattered piece of clothing back then. But I was already running late and had no time to open up the stitches and sew again.

Now came the most uncomfortable part. To reach the newspaper vendor, I would have to pass several relatives' houses, including that of the uncle who had thrown us out. Embarrassed that my family members would tease and deride me if they were to see me in torn clothes, I stretched out my palm down on the patch, trying to conceal it, while walking on the opposite side of the road passing Uncle Sanjeev's house. On my return, I held the newspaper to cover the focal point of my awkwardness in the hope that no one would spot the frayed cloth. That day, the walk through Karkala's main market road to the paper vendor seemed never-ending. The fact, as I understood much later in life when I mulled over these incidents, was that nobody had noticed me in my collaged shorts. Nobody would have bothered to cast so much as a glance in my direction. I was so mortified of being ridiculed that I never lifted my eyes off the ground. Poverty and the shame born of it can fill one with complex emotions. The acute feeling of humiliation was entirely in my head.

The money that we earned barely met our daily expenses. Buying clothes was a luxury. Owing to our financial situation, we could not afford to buy new cloth material. I bought a new pair of shorts only once a year, during Ugadi (the Hindu New Year festival). One can only imagine my state when Mother fell ill in such poor conditions—it was a nightmare. For treatment, doctors admitted her in a government hospital where medical facilities were heavily subsidised. Even so, I needed to pay a small amount for her discharge. I did not know what to do.

I was walking to the hospital on the day I was to bring her home. To my luck, I chanced upon a ten-rupee note by the roadside. It was covered in dirt and appeared to have been lying there unobserved for quite a while. I knew that the money would help me tide over many problems we were facing at the time. I picked it up and waited for some time, hoping that the person who had lost it would come looking. Interestingly, the money had fallen in front of a shop called Stylo, a store selling readymade garments.

Some childhood fascinations are everlasting. Impressed by the name Stylo (it could be because I struck some luck here), I named my very first salon, the one I opened in Thane, 'Shiva's Stylo'. The same holds true with my first motorbike. I bought a Royal Enfield Bullet only because the supervisors in the coffee estates used a similar two-wheeler. Besotted, I would stand and stare at the motorbike. Later, my dream of owning a similar make was fulfilled when I was ready to buy a vehicle of my own.

That day, when I found the money in front of the shop called Stylo, that single note made all the difference to our lives. The money helped me pay up the dues at the hospital while getting my mother discharged. With the remaining money, we purchased other essentials such as an aluminium water pot and a jute rope, materials needed to draw out water from our only source—the well. The rope we had been using was in tatters and the pot sported several holes. It was quite a funny sight whenever we drew water; nearly half of it would seep out of the holes, like little fountains, falling back into the well.

Such was the extent of our tragic circumstances. To meet our requirement of two pots of water, we would have to draw out four or five pots, until we had sufficient water for the day. Weary after drawing pot after pot of water, my mother's palms would be scarred with boils and cuts.

Death Knell

Kariminabai was aware that I had no qualms in doing manual labour. So one day, she sent me down the well to clean the bottom pit. I was reluctant to go simply because I was terribly scared. But to whom could I complain? Could I refuse? It was part of our unstated deal with Kariminabai in exchange for her hospitality, and our biggest need was a roof above our heads.

I dreaded stepping down the deep dark well. There were narrow steps at the circular edge of the stone wall to get to the base with a rope tied to a bucket. I clutched on to this rope for dear life. The bucket was provided to fill dirt collected at the bed of the well and to clear blocked ducts of natural springs so that clean water could gradually fill up the well once the process was complete. I would have to pile up muck in the bucket while Kariminabai's family members drew it up, threw the dirt and rolled it down again. Two other men who tried to get down to the bottom abandoned the task halfway and climbed back to the top. I had no such choice.

As I started to step down the well, the air felt easy to breathe. I took one step at a time, gingerly placing my foot on the stone. The walls were moist and wet in parts, covered with tiny delicate leaves of the Hamsapadi plant. Incidentally, tender and artistically shaped, these leaves are used for medicinal and decorative purposes on greeting cards in their dried form, not in villages but, surprisingly, in urban locales. I wondered how those pretty-looking leaves could grow in a dark dungeon-like hole, where sunlight barely crept in. But then, nature's beauty is seen in the most unlikely places.

As I descended further, brushing against a host of spider webs that almost blinded my vision, the air began to get stuffy. The light was faint. Shadowy images of swaying weeds on the wall raised my fears manifold. Deeper into the well, the day appeared to be changing gradually into night and the darkness enveloped me. I felt my palms sweating, my body was soaked with perspiration and my heart was beating fast. I tried to keep a strong foothold, gripping another stone step by curling my toes around its edge. By now, I was beginning to slip on the wet thick moss emerging from the well's crevices.

Every foot down felt like stepping on a path leading straight to death. Putting one wrong foot forward, I feared, would be fatal. I died a thousand deaths climbing down those hundred-odd steps to reach the base. I was in a do-or-die kind of situation. I was compelled to complete the inexorable journey though.

With avowed determination, I chose to complete the task I had committed myself to. This attitude of steely determination has been a way of life for me and my primary philosophy whenever I am faced with a challenge. No problem then seems insurmountable to me. *Where there is a will, there is a way...* I thoroughly believe in this dictum.

My mother was filled with sadness that I was made to get down the well because only she could empathise with the fear I had within me. '*They would never spare you, would they? They made you go right down to the bottom of the well when I was at work,*' she spoke in a voice choked with misery that night as we sat on the floor together to have our dinner.

She imagined the terror that the ordeal must have put into my mind while going down the well. '*What if I had lost you?*' she sobbed and asked. I had no answer to that because I could still taste the crippling fear I had felt earlier that day. My mother also said that if she had been at home, she would not have granted permission to let me go down into the well. Years later, it still is a memory that leaves me frozen.

Odd Jobs—Farmer, Milkman, Dung-maker

Even before I could dive headlong into salon work as a young boy, I was doing an assortment of odd jobs. In a rural setup, these jobs were most elementary but required an immense amount of manual labour. Beginning with collecting cowdung, tending to cattle, feeding and grazing them, selling milk in the market, farming, cultivating vegetables and fruits and selling the produce—it was an endless toil. As a child, I learnt to plough the field with my grandfather in our ancestral home at Nitte. The place, located on the outskirts of Mangalore, thanks to growing urbanisation, is now within city limits and a well-known educational centre.

Reprocessing cowdung was one chore that no member in the family volunteered for because no one wanted to get their hands dirtied. So at a young age, since my family was 'doing us a favour' by giving us shelter, I learnt to make dung patty, which in its dried form is used as fuel, and in the wet form, is used to clean and swab floors in village homes. I would collect dung in a pit by mixing hay and water to make simple manure for farming processes.

The other long-drawn process of making farmyard manure was using dung and the leaves of a plant called *Gliricidia Sepium*. Locally, it is simply called *gobbara soppu*—gobbara meaning manure and soppu meaning leaves. These tall and leafy trees are planted on the borders of farms and used primarily for manure-making. Their leaves fix nitrogen, an essential component of compost and needed for in growing crops. I was taught to make this manure in three layers—mud soil as a base, some gravel and sand scattered over it to create porosity in the mixture and in the top layer, the soppu leaves, other plant waste and cowdung. The same process was repeated layer on layer and kept for weeks to form organic manure. I had to keep a watchful eye on these formations. I also assisted in making dung pats and dung cakes, which were used as fuel for cooking and to boil bath water.

Sweet-toothed Tales of Shiva and Krishna

While engaged in doing errands, sometimes I liked to indulge in tomfoolery, the kind that harmed nobody. I was just a little boy having some fun. Along with my cousin Krishna, perhaps the only person I have emotionally connected with since childhood, I would plan to approach handcart vendors who looked for helpers to push the heavily loaded carts from the rear end. When somebody pushed the cart from the back, it became easier to manually pull it from the front.

There was a reason why I would seek only those cart-pullers who carried jaggery. Not only were we paid money for the errand and rewarded with a handful of sweet jaggery after the task, but in the course of pushing the cart, we would also nibble at and siphon off some of it, bit by bit, into our pockets. I was the naughtier of the two, and Krishna, always the softie, merely followed my instructions. By the end of our expedition, we would always have a huge helping of the sweet. Thrilled with our little loot, we would run into the fields, rest under a huge tree and feast to our heart's content.

Both of us enjoyed gatecrashing weddings where the food served would be sumptuous. We knew all the venues and temples in Karkala where weddings were held during an auspicious time of the year and looked forward to enjoying a hearty meal accompanied by a delicious selection of sweets, the payasam (sweet dessert made of rice or lentils) being our favourite. We never stayed long enough to be caught out for our mischief by family members from the bride or groom. Before anyone could notice us, we would run away from the premises.

Day-long rituals at temples called for another round of walking in to show that we were partaking in ceremonies, but we would actually go there to gorge on the delicious lunch served. We would be the uninvited guests among hundreds of people and would slip out before the priests suspected our intentions and called our bluff.

At other times, we would creep midway into the night-long Yakshagana recital—a musical opera on Indian epics and mythological stories—performed inside temporary tents set up on village grounds. We always slipped in late, and not from the front door, for fear of being asked to pay for tickets, but from the sides of the temporarily fixed tents. Inside, we would squat on the floor, watch the performances for a while, and then, despite the high pitch at which musicians played drums, danced and sang songs, we would unwittingly fall asleep, only to be woken up by the organisers the next morning.

Small pleasures indeed, but they made us happy.

Some of my most memorable moments were spent with Krishna. We still share a strong bond as first cousins. When we meet in Karkala, where Krishna runs a salon, we muse over our childhood days and become two playful kids all over again. He is my maternal aunt's son, the aunt who is closest to my mother. Krishna had joined me for some time in Mumbai. Together we worked in a few salons in Ghatkopar and stayed in the slums of Ramabai colony.

For a while, we ran an eatery on a handcart where we sold dosas and fresh lime juice late in the night after finishing work at the salon in Ghatkopar. This business, set up to help one of our cousins, Shivanna, did well, since it was patronised by late-night moviegoers, hotel staff and industrial workers who preferred to have a meal before embarking on a long local train journey home.

One night, we allowed Shivanna to push the cart as we

walked behind him on a path that had an incline. All of a sudden, the careless man lost his grip on the handcart, letting it wheel down the small bridge in full speed to bang into a parked car, breaking the vehicle's glass windows. We had to wind up our business after paying damages to the car owner.

My Favourite Fruit

For me, no job was too small or too trivial as long as there was honesty and integrity in it. I took to the task like a thorough professional. I knew that I faced limitations because of my lack of formal education. I was not fortunate to walk into offices equipped with the mandated qualifications for a job. And so, all that I absorbed from my environment, I would put to practice.

My knowledge of reading and writing too was elementary since I had dropped out midway in school. It was a big accomplishment for me to earn a tiny sum of one paisa; this denomination may not be in use today and perhaps even unheard of for today's generation, but it held a lot of value in my young days. Imagine my plight when I lost a twenty-five-paisa coin, also known as four annas, while travelling between two villages, Kabettu and Attur, for a job. It was an enormous amount for more reasons than one.

Back then, I had to cycle a distance of 2.5 kilometres one way, but midway, I would stop to treat myself to a luscious, sweet and sour local fruit called *jaarige.* There was this huge tree on an open, sandy ground by the road. Further away, the tract was surrounded by trees and hills. I would park the cycle against the tree trunk, play around and jump about on the sandy patch around it. I would pick up stones and fling them high to hit my target and then would wait to catch them one by one before they hit the ground. Then sitting under the same tree, I would bite into the fruit's juicy pulp. The tangy taste still feels so real that my mouth waters at the thought of it.

Whenever I recollect the amount of effort and time I spent aiming to get this delicious fruit from the treetop, it feels like it merited all the hard work that one would devote to winning a reward. However, these days, fewer jaarige trees can be sighted compared to my childhood days when more of them were grown in the rural outback. During visits to my hometown nowadays, I try to source these juicy fruits from the few farmers who grow them in their fields.

One day, as usual, I flung a stone at a fruit hanging high on the tree and I heard the sound of metal hitting a stone below. Confused, I stopped and checked my pocket. To my horror, I realised that a coin which I had kept inside my pocket had slipped out of a tiny hole, since the hand-stitched threads of my pocket had frayed and given way. Aghast, I searched desperately for the coin, but my efforts were in vain. Over the next three days, I visited the same place again and again, rummaging the area, digging my hands into the sand, pulling out weeds, casting away pebbles and upturning stones, just to find that lost coin. Alas, I had lost it forever.

The Crow Who Stole My Sister's Happiness

In school, twice a week, we were provided snacks, and those days were looked forward to with immense anticipation by all the children. It used to be a tasty meal, slightly spicy, made out of semolina, locally known as *shajjige*, or more commonly, upma. I relished eating it so much that I would carry some of it home in a tiffin box to share it with my little sister. Boys in school would tease me about the box. But the little girl back home would jump and clap in glee every time I fed her with shajjige. I would wait to watch this moment of pure joy, and her thrill made everything worth it.

One day, I forgot to carry the box and I could not get the snack packed. So I went to a local eatery, bought the same snack, wrapped it in a packet and took a brisk walk home. All the while, I held the packet in my right hand, hoisting it above my shoulder. But it was not to be. A black-winged creature snatched my sister's source of joy right out of my hands!

A crow had come flying overhead, pecked at the food and swooped away with the packet even before I could react to the misdemeanour. I ran after it, taking big strides and calling out to the crow, but it obviously did not care.

Shocked and bewildered, I froze in my tracks. I stood there as it rose higher and higher, finally becoming a tiny black speck in the clear blue sky. The packet seemed to appear tinier and tinier, held aloft in the pointed beak of the crow, almost disappearing from my sight. I kept staring at it in the hope that the packet would slip down the crow's beak and I would pick it up and run home. I felt giddy craning my neck to catch the last black dot of the bird that stole my sister's happiness.

This incident is imprinted on my mind like a mark made with indelible ink. Whenever I see a crow, it brings memories of my sister, whom I loved dearly. We played games, frolicked together, bonded in grief and fun; she was my buddy even though she could not have understood anything about the grave family intrigues going on around us. Our problems were alike. We shared food and wore scant clothes. I remember her as a baby, unclothed all the time. Other babies in the household wore frocks, pyjamas and jumpers.

I felt lonely when she passed away at the age of four. Among the three of us—my mother, sister and me—she bore the brunt of our poverty. I feel guilty about that. She was suffering from water retention, her skin was scaling, and added to that, she was denied essential nutrition in our dire circumstances. We could not afford to treat her ailment either. She died due to negligence.

First they ignore you, then they laugh at you,
then they fight you, then you win.

—*Mahatma Gandhi, Father of the Nation*

chapter three

FROM BARBER TO LEADING COIFFEUR

My Work, My Passion

To me, work is worship. It is spiritual; it is my faith and my religion.

I believe that when heart and soul are put into work, everything falls into place. Life is never going to be easy. The path will be laden with difficulties. Give as much as you can to your work, put in hundred percent effort, and the returns will be doubled or tripled.

I have never been embarrassed or lazy about taking up any kind of work, no matter how difficult, menial or laborious the job.

As a barber, I learnt to hone my skills with sheer practice. I pursued the craft by undertaking a few courses abroad in one of the best academies in the world. This enabled me to evolve as a creative designer.

Most relatives expressed doubts about my efforts. They made snide comments: 'Arre… What are you learning? What will you do in the future?' Others made disparaging sounds of criticism: 'Chee… Chee…!'

I would maintain a solemn silence. But my thoughts would be agitated: 'What! Am I holding soiled cloth? What is wrong with this profession?'

But not one to be intimidated by people's comments, I made an effort to explain my feelings about my profession. I wondered why young boys in our community were ashamed to be known as barbers. They were opting for a different field of work, hoping to gain respect in society.

'This is genuine work. It requires skill, art and talent. There is honesty and dedication in it,' I tried to explain. In fact, it is common knowledge that for several generations, our community, called Bhandary, has been associated with this line of work—cutting hair and shaving beards. Old, family-run shops are usually ordinary places set up on the wayside, with modest interiors fitted with wooden chairs. The better ones have laminated tables and gaudy plastic covers with large mirrors. Back then, they catered exclusively to males, although children were also brought to these salons by family elders.

Conventionally, barbers played a crucial role in society. They were emissaries to kings, resolved conflicts as they were good messengers, played matchmakers and, most importantly, they were adept at playing instruments in music bands. At one time, the tradition was to have a haircut or a shave done early in the morning or before 11.00 a.m. at the most. Therefore, customers visited barber shops before noon. The rest of the day, barbers chose to be gainfully occupied, playing music with bands performing at weddings. They specialised in playing drums and popular instruments like the shehnai and the nadaswaram. In Palimaru village, a close relative has a board outside the shop saying, 'Hairstylist and Saxophonist'. Some pictures in old historical books depict barbers performing minor surgeries as well as practising dentistry. A barber's role in society and his work have come a long way from a mixed bag of duties and obligations.

I learnt to operate the barber's razor blade by testing the tool on my own skin in order to gain perfection while using it on my clients. I continued to practise by shaving my arms and legs until I was able to run the blade in a smooth fashion over my body. When I was sure of my work, I shaved the beard of a twenty-four-year-old estate labourer; it was his first time too. He had just a few strands, but with regular shaving, he aimed to have a thick beard. I was apprehensive about running the razor on his soft and tender skin, but he was adamant and I went along. Thankfully, all went well.

Call me a coiffeur, a hair designer, a hair dresser or a businessman, it is just a matter of perception. If you do good work with all your heart and soul, you can see God, and if you do not, then perhaps you see the Devil. I have tremendous love and passion for my work. I developed my skills by pushing myself to perfection, and that is the reason I share an intimate relationship with hair. It may seem unusual, but as soon as I begin to work on a client's head, examining the hair and deciding on the cut, I get the feeling that the locks begin to interact with me, guiding me to chop in a certain way, and the eventual result is a haircut that best suits the client.

When my customers feel satisfied after a haircut, it gives me immense satisfaction that I have been instrumental in giving them happiness. Being a hairdresser has given me the opportunity to meet some well-known and distinguished personalities. A coiffeur's place is not just in a salon, but in people's minds and hearts too. For instance, we remember the doctor when we are ill. However, I would say we remember our hairstylist every time we look at our reflection in the mirror. The fact is that a hairstyle creates a personal bond with a customer; they become friends over snips and trims.

I developed a passion for my work at a very early age. When I was thirteen, the former prime minister, Indira Gandhi, campaigned for the Chikamagalur by-election seat after her defeat in Rae Bareilly post the nearly two-year-long emergency she had imposed in the country. There was a festive spirit in the air, with buntings, posters and flower garlands decorating the podium where she was to deliver her speech. The entire village was excited about her arrival. Peasants, farmers and the working class gathered in huge numbers to listen to her.

The period between 1975 and 1977 is seen as the darkest period post-Independence. In the tiny village of Yelemadalu, where feudal lords reigned over poor peasants, exploitation was rampant. People were used to restrictions and constraints imposed on their way of life. It made no difference to them if Mrs Gandhi put the clamp or not. They were, on the contrary, quite in awe of her and admired her for acquiring huge expanses of land held by the wealthy, and distributing the same to the poor. Even as the entire country opposed Mrs Gandhi's autocratic way of functioning, villagers regarded her as a mother to the poor. After all, their only source of news was the humble radio that would air government broadcasts.

I went to have a close look at her during the stopover campaign, the place being close to our salon. What caught my eye was her side-swept shock of silver-grey bouffant that conferred on her a distinct aura of regality. I was so enamoured by her stately hairdo that in my boyish naivety, I stood there imagining how I would have styled her bob to retain that sense of power she exuded. She looked authoritative and fully in control. People worshipped her like a goddess. I let the creative ideas flow in my head, assessing numerous styles that would match her position of being the most important person in the country.

Hunting the Wild Sheep

The gurgling river across Uncle's house at Yelemandalu was my only solace in hours of sadness. This is the same place where I bathed, washed clothes and played in cold, flowing streams. The entire place was quite mesmerising and soothing to the senses.

I would gaze admiringly at the reflection of tall bamboo trees in the water. The cane shoots looked far taller than they actually were. Lying on the rocks, I would watch ripples, small and large, formed by leaves kissing the water when a gentle breeze swept by. Bent branches of trees reclined low on the water surface, their dried leaves swaying, floating in the stream.

The silent sentinels of the woodlands were timber logs partly stuck in the water course and along the periphery. I got the feeling they knew everything that was happening around, in the deep forest, in the waters and on land.

Nature's calming aura always perked up my mood. I jumped on rocks, played with fish in bubbling streams, scooped out algae and sat over one log and then the other, imagining that it was my ship on which I could sail away to a safer shore. I dived to catch fish with my bare hands, and when I did, I would experience a feeling of elation. I never felt the need to cast a hook, line or sinker even in icy cold waters. The local hunter, Kuppanna, used a fish hook to catch his bait. When he saw me diving headlong into the water, he let out a throaty laugh, looking at my eagerness to catch them live. I had that childlike exuberance in me. And when I felt somebody was nice to me, I would go all out to please the person. Kuppanna was one such man. I was like his Man Friday, assisting him in hunting expeditions to the closest forest by carrying his bag, torch, gas-lit lantern, searchlight and flask.

Wearing hunter boots, a bowler hat, a searchlight on his forehead and a rifle on his shoulder, he marched into the darkness while I followed him barefoot in my shorts. I was filled with the enthusiasm to tag along because, to me, his kindness was overwhelming. One night, he shot at a beefy-looking sheep running into the dense jungle area. Before packing for the night, he briefed me about the track his prey would take, roughly earmarking the area where it would collapse.

Dropping off the hunter's paraphernalia at his home, I turned back into the forest to track the animal. I found the bleeding sheep in the bush. Huge and heavy in comparison to my tiny self, it was a struggle for me as I dragged the enormous animal to a bush closer to the village border and covered it with leaves, away from prying eyes. The next morning, I took the hunter to his prized catch. Utterly shocked and impressed with my effort, he patted my back. Walking back home, I felt like I had conquered the world. Such appreciation was rare. Later, the village people shared the animal's meat.

The reason I am mentioning this example is to elucidate that whenever I make up my mind to do something, I pursue it to the end, against all odds, until I am successful. My cousins often used to brag about tasting fruit salad in a particular shop in Karkala's main market. I understood that if they were showing off, then it might be a unique experience, costing quite a sum. I did not possess enough money to splurge on food indulgences. All my meals were cooked at home and I never visited a restaurant or an eatery to taste an item. Only the affluent class was known to spend on such luxuries.

I had heard that a fruit salad was a mixture of fruits topped with loads of cashewnuts. So I came up with a plan.

On the outskirts of the town was a cashew orchard. I picked up a number of cashews that had fallen on the ground and sold them to a grocer at the market. With that money, I visited the fruit parlour and tasted a bowl of the much talked-about dessert—the fruit salad—and finally satiated my palate.

It is a different story that when my uncles and cousins heard about my little escapade (in small towns, such incidents were promptly discussed and reported), they gave me a mouthful of abuse. Sarcastically, they asked if a poor boy like me was aping the wealthy by cultivating expensive tastes. I wondered what was wrong in my gathering cashewnuts and selling them for a small price. It had taken me hours to collect a good amount of cashews scattered on the ground. I thought that I had earned my treat.

Eating cashew, jackfruit or mango was considered the prerogative of well-off people. The poor were fortunate to eat them when the rich offered to share a part of it from their basket. I have some fond memories of feasting on jackfruit as a child at my grandfather's town Nitte, and to date, I relish the fruit. We were taught to tap on the fruit to check its variety and readiness to be eaten.

If the sound went 'dub… dub…' upon tapping, the fruit would be soft inside and ready to eat, and if the sound went 'tak… tak…', then the fruit would be firm inside. Merely spotting a jackfruit tree and its spiked skinned fruit hanging on the bark at the bottom of the tree evokes a sense of nostalgia. It puts a smile on my face even today.

I learned that courage was not the absence of fear,
but the triumph over it. The brave man is
not he who does not feel afraid,
but he who conquers that fear.

—Nelson Mandela, South Africa's first black president who followed the non-violent path in his anti-apartheid movement

chapter four

TYRANT UNCLE

Job of a Scarecrow

It may have been the hottest day that summer. But summers have always been the warmest in the coastal village of Palimaru, roughly sixteen kilometres from Karkala. At the time, I was staying with my maternal aunt's son-in-law Sesu Bhandary and his wife Yamuna. I assisted him in the cycle repair shop and also hawked vegetables, grown in their kitchen garden, on his behalf.

Two-wheelers fascinated me, and the ones in closest proximity were bicycles. There was a small cycle at the shop that seemed almost tailor-made for my height of about 4.5 feet. I would enjoy riding this run-down yet faithful steed through the village alleyways. On a medium-sized cycle, I even tried a wheelie late in the night on an unlit jagged path, and as you can guess, I tumbled over and injured myself. Cuts, bruises and injuries were a routine part of my life. I would dust away the mud granules and quickly get on my feet to resume riding. The joy of cycling was exhilarating. I would continue to paddle for as long as I wished.

After watching feats played out in circus shows, I would try to emulate extraordinary challenges performed by artistes (usually village folk) on cycles for prize money. For example, I was fascinated by the man who would cycle nonstop for nearly ten days without getting off the wheels. He brushed his teeth, had meals and even rested on the cycle itself, excusing himself from it perhaps only to answer nature's call. And as a ritual, every morning was an opportunity for me to try out similar acrobatic stunts on a cycle in the premises of a nearby temple.

This temple had a fairly large ground surrounded by a cluster of tall trees, including the widely grown *Moringa Oleifera*, or what we commonly know as drumstick, or *nuggekaayi* in Kannada. The long sticks, one of my favourite foods, filled with juicy pulp and seeds, are a must in the preparation of sambar. It is an accompanying dish, which I relish having for breakfast with dosa or idli.

I remember soulful renditions reverberating in the air from the shrine's loudspeaker. Bhajans invoking a pantheon of Hindu gods, Lord Ganesha in particular (I distinctly remember his idol), would play in the background as I rode the cycle for nearly an hour. The music always drowned out the chirruping of birds, but once the music stopped, the twittering would rise to a new crescendo. While cycling, I would savour this confluence of nature's own musical notes. And finally, exhausted after an invigorating play of wheels around the temple, I would head home.

Three months passed by in the village quite peacefully. But destiny had other plans. My kind of fun was short-lived.

One day, as I sat wiping profuse sweat off the brow while tinkering with an old broken wheel in the shop, I heard a familiar gruff voice call out to me. Turning back, I saw a giant-like figure walking in my direction from the far end of the tiled shed that housed half-a-dozen old cycles. These were leased to customers on an hourly basis. As the figure approached, the silhouette in the sun grew clearer. It was my paternal uncle Govind Bhandary. He had come from the hilly tracts of Yelemadalu, travelling down to Palimaru, and I was sure he had not trekked the distance only to meet me casually. Earlier, I had spent my summer holidays at this uncle's house, assisting him in his salon. Knowing the man, I suspected there would be a specific purpose to this visit.

Dragging a wooden stool, he made himself comfortable and began to speak in a low voice, enquiring after my work at the repair shop. In soft, gentle tones, he tried to talk me into going with him to his village so that he could train me in haircutting. Despite the seemingly tentative pitch, his voice demanded that I had better follow his command. It was rather apparent that he was not seeking my consent. Uncle, my father's younger brother, was a headstrong man who always considered his own decision final, and one had no choice but to meekly abide.

To take him for his word was risky. But he made a veiled promise to part with my father's share of the family property and hand it over to my mother. Now that was a carrot dangling in front of me.

My face lit up. I thought it would benefit me to learn a new skill rather than doing odd jobs at a repair shop. It was quickly settled that I would live with his family at his house, while my mother would stay back at Karkala as Kariminabai's tenant and continue to stitch clothes for a living.

I travelled with Uncle to the cold climes of Yelemadalu, hoping to give a constructive direction to my life. Little did I know that the next four years, well almost, at Uncle's place would change my life forever. They turned out to be the worst years of my life. But today, as I look back at those horrifying days, I feel it was God's way of preparing me to cope with the uncertainties that may arise in future. Those experiences made me a stronger person emotionally, taught me to read human character, and effectively laid out the path for a coiffeur's career.

But in my early teens, I did not realise how deviously a family elder could play out his shenanigans on a naive young boy. And, because I had tagged along with a lot of hope, I was in for an even ruder shock. I should have been prepared, I suppose. I could not believe that my first task, a menial one at that, was to become a scarecrow!

My uncle's residence was a scenic house located on a hillock. It was built on a slope consisting of three levels—the steps leading up to the hillock, then a garden, and a little further, at the top, the house. It had an uneven fence outlining the boundary made of bamboo and wild shrubs. Being a wintry landscape, it used to be chilly there most times of the year, with cold winds blowing dried petals and leaves into the farmhouse. I could not resist jumping to catch floating, cotton-ball-like clouds that appeared to be hanging in mid-air. Gliding from the hill, they would drift into the house from the back door and sway gently out of the front exit.

In an area covering two acres of land, Uncle cultivated flowers, fruits, vegetables and grains, and sold them at the doorstep of his salon. A cowshed and a poultry farm in the backyard added to the numerous sources of income he had set up. He made a good profit by selling the milk of more than half-a-dozen cows.

The day we reached, I helped him with planting tomatoes on a patch at the side. For days ahead, my task included keeping a watch on new shoots. When red blobs of tiny tomatoes popped out of the buds, Uncle feared that the sprightly blooms might face an attack from birds and insects. So he got impatient and turned me into a scarecrow!

I had to sit amidst the greens and sprouting red dots with a gunnysack over me to shoo away birds such as crows that were hovering around to peck and maul the luscious fruit.

Struggling inside the coarse jute cloth for nearly ten hours every day, I would drive away all winged creatures. Shoo... hush... hush... whoosh! Shoo... hush... hush... whoosh! I kept yelling from dawn to dusk, straining my vocal chords.

After I had successfully driven away birds from tomatoes, my next assignment was to crouch in the middle of a patch producing underground shoots like sweet potatoes. Flies and insects would swarm at the sweet saplings and drain my energy as I ran to swoop over them with a stick. Beans, aubergines, gourds, peppers, corn, okra and melons, all growing above the ground level, called for different capabilities in shooing away pests. I had to bend my back in an awkward manner to scatter sawdust pest repellent on plants that were neither tall nor tiny, but mid-height, like stunted trees. For guava and chikkoo trees, long and thick thorny sticks were tied to branches to prevent owls from hanging on them at night.

Rodents were a huge menace, and the customers' chopped hair was put to good use. The waste was stuffed in ground holes to trap rats.

I had to dart up and down the small hill, leaping over the coarsely laden stones that formed the steps to the house, while moving lightly in a swathe of roses, jasmine, chrysanthemum and hibiscus flowers, and jostling among guava, jackfruit, drumstick and dwarf coconut trees. In short, I would be running and gasping over the entire horticultural patch several times a day to keep at bay all feathered flock and nature's living organisms that hungrily eyed the crop.

Uncle's grand plan of dragging me out of the cycle shop now began to dawn on me.

The salon, being the sole outlet in the village and adjoining areas, had a steady flow of clients. To manage all the work on his own was wearing my uncle out. His children, two daughters who stayed at their grandparents' house, and another daughter and a year-old baby boy who were with him, were too young to be put to labour. The miser that he was, Uncle refused to hire help. He needed someone to slog over daily chores. I was young, sturdy and ever-willing to work. Yes, I worked all day and how—toiling in the soil, dirtying my hands and legs, being bitten and gnawed by creepy-crawly insects.

At 5.30 a.m., the sound of cock-a-doodle-doo would wake up the entire family, including the baby. Uncle had set a schedule for me—by 6.00 a.m., I had to clean the cowshed, throw dung into a large pit to make manure, carry fodder and water to the cattle, and then let them off to graze their way into green fields on the outskirts of the village. As the cattle ambled in the meadows, for the next two hours I had to cycle for about six kilometres to deliver milk to people's homes in and around the village, in huge tin cans hanging from the handlebar and in the carrier behind.

Using an adult male bicycle proved a challenge, as my legs could never reach the pedals if I chose to ride from the seat. Adult male bicycles have a bar-rod fixed from the handle to the seat, in case a child would like to ride along. At the repair shop, I had learnt to ride by keeping my left foot on the left pedal and sliding the right foot from under the bar-rod onto the right pedal. I managed to cycle long distances with milk cans in tow pretty well.

My next task was to rush to the salon to dust, sweep and swab before Uncle got there in the morning. I would have similarly cleaned the place the previous night before closing the salon, but a wash-up in the morning was a necessity. Through the day, I assisted in catering to clients and in selling fruits and vegetables. Midway through the day, I had to get back to water the garden of fruits and vegetables. Before sundown, I went scampering barefoot to the fields, calling out to the cattle by their names to get them home.

Kamalakshi...iiii... Sundari...iiii...Ammanni... iiii...

Ammi…iiii… I kept shouting out their names, scurrying over the lush terrain, battling hordes of other cattle belonging to other farmers.

Hearing my voice, the animals would come darting towards me and I would goad them home with a stick, steering them down hillocks, across fields and through the narrow tar road, dodging a stray tractor or a tempo coming our way. Back in the shed, I fed them with fodder and water, and helped my aunt in milking them again in the evening.

The cowshed, located at the rear end of the slightly inclined plot, had cows roped to a long log of wood in a series, and the wooden shed had a separate gate for cattle movement. Close by, a dump served as a mixing pit for dung and various dried and fresh leaves to make plant manure. One such common variety was made of the leaves of gobbara soppu. Cowdung's most utilitarian purpose is fuel; sun-baked, flat or round pieces kept fire embers burning for long hours in the oven for activities such as cooking and heating bath water. Even rice broth for cattle was cooked with the help of dung patty.

Fowl had a little world of their own. Chickens frolicked in the backyard while colour-spangled hens and roosters in yellow, green and blue rested atop the tiled roof or on tree branches. They would climb down from their reaches as the sun set in the horizon, but sometimes they liked to play longer, in which case, I had to literally entrap them by flinging a wet towel, so that their legs would freeze with dampness. Holding the still-quacking creatures in my arms, I would huddle the rest into their dwellings also called *koli goodu* (chicken coops), built out of mud.

This being the daily grind, work went on for months on end without a penny paid for my services. Uncle did not show any inclination to teach me haircutting as he had promised. Nor was he satisfied with the tasks I was performing as per his diktats. He was a cruel taskmaster, utterly rude and downright obnoxious. His other traits, none of the praiseworthy kind, included being foul-mouthed, forever shouting, screaming and throwing a fit, without any provocation.

Vanishing Spirit

Ostensibly taken to be trained in haircutting, I was turned into some sort of a bonded labourer toiling in the cowshed, cultivating and selling fruits and vegetables, cleaning the salon and, only much later, assisting him in his work. These were the several sources of income that made my uncle a prosperous man. Yet, he never paid me a salary nor did he think I deserved a reward even by way of a small gift. I had just one pair of khaki shorts and a shirt; he gave me a new pair once a year, during the Ugadi festival. To make matters worse, he began to splurge on country liquor, a habit that gradually became a vice.

He was wary of taking the bottle home; it was hidden in the salon. After winding up the day's work at sundown, he took a few swigs. The practice thus continued clandestinely for some time, since he may not have wanted to drink in my aunt's presence. As time passed, he guzzled more and more in the salon, walking back home in a drunken stupor. Later, he began carrying the bottle home, regardless of what anyone thought. A large stock was stashed away in the salon as well.

Eventually, drinking became a daily habit and with that, his behaviour took an aggressive and violent turn. Showering expletives like *sulemaga* or *bollimaga* (son of a whore/son of a bitch), commonly used in Kannada and Tulu, he would abuse everyone around until he fell asleep. He also started beating me with a bamboo cane.

I was an easy target, available at hand for him to rain down all the pent-up frustration and resentment he may have harboured in life. Arrogance was in his nature, he had never been a kind man. But after drinking and losing his senses, he changed into an even more horrendous creature.

Ironically, the liquor that he guzzled every day had to be fetched by me. What could be weirder! I had to walk long distances to bring him the local brew. Every week I would trek four kilometres back and forth, opting for a shorter route through the forest area, for a homemade brew brought from the temple priest Vasu's house. Once the heady concoction went to his head, he would kick up a ruckus and abuse, starting with beating up his wife and finally caning me until he was totally exhausted.

As part of my duty, I had to clean up the salon before locking it at the end of the day. Uncle would take leave early in the evening. In between sweeping and swabbing the place, I was tempted to take a few sips from the hidden liquor bottle. After swallowing some, I would top it up with drinking water so that the quantity appeared unchanged. In a few days, Uncle did find something amiss while sipping the liquor, but could not quite figure out the diluted potion. The same pattern continued. I would sip bit by bit every evening, and the liquid would become thinner and thinner as the brew began to reduce in quantity.

Annoyed with the watered-down drink, he would remark, '*Vasu's brew is getting bad day after day. Not the fine quality it used to be.*' He never did realise that the heady potion was mixed with water. The spirit was not vanishing into thin air. I would smile secretly, turning to face a blank wall to hide my expressions, for having managed to hoodwink him. This petty mischief gave me enormous pleasure. Strangely, it does even now, and I still smile to myself as I reminisce.

I was beginning to realise too that I was getting slightly addicted to the obnoxious-smelling liquid myself, even though it may have been just a few sips. I was doing it only as an act of defiance because Uncle enjoyed his drink. I wanted to deny him what he liked most. It was my way of getting even with him. But, before it became my problem, I decided to put a stop to it.

Meanwhile, Uncle's addiction was turning into a severe problem; he took the bottle home and continued to drink after dinner. The more he drank, the more brutally he behaved. In an inebriated state, he would physically torture his wife—once she threatened to jump into the well—and beat up his young daughter. Could he spare me? I was always in the direct line of fire; with a cane in hand, he would chase me around the house and the compound. When he did catch up, he would give me the thrashing of my life, rendering my body black and blue. The wound marks he gifted me—a gash on my chin and a deep cut on my lip—are still there on my body.

Screaming, shouting and swearing, he would continue pasting me with the cane until he felt drained out. Bruised by repeated assaults, I would fall asleep without so much as applying any medication over my bruises. At times, my aunt gave me a homemade turmeric paste, an antiseptic. It helped to heal the physical injuries.

I figured out that my uncle was doing well financially. He was earning more than what he did prior to my arrival because now he had extra hands to take over the manual labour. With money accruing from various sources, arrogance overtook his sense of propriety.

Queasy Ghost!

One of the most frightful days of my childhood was when a schoolteacher died hanging by a rope in the salon's neighbourhood at Yelemadalu. The teacher lived alone in a house that consisted of only one room. His family lived in another village, and his wife and children would visit during vacations.

Even as the death created chaos in the area, curious villagers gathered outside the forty-two-year-old man's house which was under police scrutiny. People began gossiping nineteen to the dozen, saying there were problems in the family life of the teacher, who taught at the primary school across the road. What those problems were, nobody knew. They discussed various reasons that might have stressed him out so as to make him take his own life ultimately.

This incident rattled me no end. Village folk, mostly Uncle's friends, tried to scare me by telling me that while I was asleep, the teacher's ghost would try to clutch my throat. Some nights, I wouldn't be able to sleep at all, literally sitting wide awake on my sleeping mat. Horrific thoughts of the spirit catching hold of my neck and strangling me to death kept haunting me. It was a strange mix of revulsion and panic.

I have always disliked touches, nudges and other gestures of overt familiarity that people indulge in even while making casual conversation. Maybe those are their ways of displaying affection or emphasising a point. For some reason, it stirs a feeling of repulsion within me. To think that a ghost would actually touch me or catch me by my neck! Horror made me queasy.

Uncle's friends continued to poke fun about the ghost's appearance. Perhaps I was the only young boy they could pull a fast one on and then snigger about it. For me, it was the one 'joke' that never seemed to die a natural death, even months after the teacher's demise. Nightmares continued to haunt me and I would sit up all night, worried sick. Unknown fears within put me in a constant state of alarm and insecurity. It embarrasses me greatly to confess that my nervousness even made me wet the mat I slept upon.

Bedwetting was shameful, yet beyond my control. As long as I stayed with Uncle Govind at Yelemadalu, up to the age of fourteen, the problem continued. At the crack of dawn, I would be up, and to my dismay, I would find that my straw mat and a cotton sheet I pulled up to cover at night would be damp and cold. Before my aunt could yell, I would scamper down to the river flowing across the road and wash the soggy mat, sheet, my shorts and bathe in freezing water.

Uncle tried to get rid of my incontinence issue, but his method of instilling fear by burning my buttocks with a hot iron ladle from the kitchen only compounded the situation. In reality, it was a medical issue, emerging as a direct consequence of mental trauma, but he had little sense to think along those lines. He believed in punishing and employing brutal tactics to resolve any crisis. Nothing stopped my problem; I continued to wet my pants every night.

At the salon, customers worried for me, expressing concern at my injuries. Some remarked that Uncle was 'not a human being, he was a strange creature'. Some others described his inhuman methods differently—'It's not blood that flows in his veins'.

Obviously, they did not see him as a normal person. Their words of sympathy would comfort me to some extent. I learnt that people were, by now, aware of his villainous ways. Some tried to advise Uncle to be kind to me. He would always snap back at them or rebuke them for trying to correct him.

Niche of Soiled Money Notes

The extent to which I was scarred for life, no one could tell. It was beyond my own comprehension too.

As the harassment meted out intensified, I began to discover my inadequacies. I began to feel that my options were limited.

After my father's death, I had had to leave school midway in order to earn. I started regretting not completing my studies. I felt a deep sense of remorse. I often pondered that if I had finished schooling and pursued further studies, perhaps I would have earned respect from people around me. I prayed for the day when I would be able to move out of that gruesome place to become independent.

Uncle and Aunt thought of me as a good-for-nothing fellow. I was made to labour worse than the local dhobi's donkey. The comparison may seem inappropriate, but I felt the mute animal's master would perhaps be more civilised than my uncle. That he would be kind enough to at least feed the donkey regular meals.

My grief was my own, and it was already manifesting its adverse effect in certain ways. Being an unusually quiet person, I rarely spoke or laughed with anyone. Never the type to start a conversation, I attempted to reply only when asked to answer. Sometimes, provocation resulted in retorts. In a way, I was becoming extremely obstinate; I would stick to my own beliefs come what may.

As for entertainment, I do not recollect doing anything to keep myself cheerful. I never had friends and never played games like most young boys did in the village. Occasionally, I joined the local kids playing cricket in the salon's compound. We used a rubber ball and substituted coconut tree branches for bats and stumps.

It troubled me to imagine what my future had in store.

In a niche between the salon's wall and roof, away from the prying eyes of Uncle, I had stashed a small amount of money earned from my earlier jobs. I stored some more in a hole dug into an unused mud oven in the salon's adjoining room, which had served as a kitchen and living area for the family before Uncle shifted to a bigger house. Some of this money was used to travel to my hometown after running away from Uncle's clutches, and some I carried with me on my first visit to Mumbai. But there was still some dough hidden in a nook in the roof.

I had stowed it away there, saving it for a rainy day. This has always been my approach towards the money I earn. I use some, spend some, and save quite a bit, thinking that some funds may be required in case of an emergency.

Years later, after setting up my business in Mumbai, when I visited Uncle at the salon, I found those currency notes, by then soiled and worn-out, tucked away in the same niche. Uncle was dumbfounded to know that there was money lying untouched for so long. He kept wondering aloud how he hadn't chanced upon the hidden treasure! He clearly did not like being outwitted, but I thoroughly enjoyed seeing him flummoxed.

Death Rites—Shaving My Head, Bathing in Icy Waters

One sunny day, I was attending to clients all by myself, since Uncle was yet to arrive at the salon. Like I mentioned, I never had wholesome meals, and that day, I had left home without breakfast. Hunger biting into my tummy, I was feeling restless. I trotted to an eatery a couple of shops away to eat dosa and sambar. I paid the eatery owner for my order—I do not recollect the amount but it was negligible. I requested him not to inform Uncle of my midday snack in his absence at the salon. But the man promptly complained. He knew that Uncle never paid me a salary, so he figured that I must have taken money from the salon's cash counter.

Back at home in the night, when confronted, I denied taking the money. Refusing to believe me, my uncle beat me up mercilessly. He wanted me to confess that instead of dropping clients' payments in the cash box, as was the practice, I pocketed some amount.

I was furious with the eatery owner, who despite being well aware of Uncle's inhuman behaviour, had chosen to tattle. In my view, I had paid up the hotel owner for what I had eaten. I expected some mercy. For working round-the-clock without any pay, I thought that I deserved a small treat, especially when my stomach was growling with hunger. Food served at home never filled my belly, for it was so little.

What followed made Uncle even more livid. I stood there resolutely, taking his thrashing without crying, shouting or even flinching. I continued standing there like a statue until he was tired of beating me.

'Look at him, how stubborn he is! I am shocked that he can put up with this kind of beating!' I overheard him telling my aunt after he had finished caning me to the point of exhaustion.

At such times, when he failed miserably and felt utterly powerless, he would ask me mockingly, 'Did you shave your head after your father died?'

He had knowingly touched a sensitive spot.

He was aware that any talk related to my father's death would break me down. The remark did evoke the desired emotion within me that day too; it was apparent from my expression. It simultaneously made me extremely emotional and angry, and I wanted to cry out loudly.

Uncle would often chide me for the hair drooping down on my forehead. I had a huge mop of forelock on the head and I liked a few strands falling loosely just above my eyes. He would threaten to catch my head and shave it bald if I did not push the hair aside. I did not like those frequent barbs targeted at shaving my head.

Hinduism calls for the son to shave his head after the death rites, in the belief that the father's soul attains a sense of completeness and finds a place in heaven. Simply put, this was Uncle's way of reminding me that I did not have a father. That he was obliging me by keeping me with him.

Once again, when he made that remark, something snapped in me—I had had enough. In a fit of anger, without thinking twice, I went running down to the stream across the road, lowered my head in the cold, gurgling water, and came charging home to Uncle with my hair soaking wet.

Bowing in front of him, I said, 'I don't remember shaving my head after the death of my father. Now you may do so. Fulfil your wish.'

This enraged him even more. 'This boy doesn't give up! I will straighten you. Where is the cane?' he hollered. Then he turned and walked away in a huff, spewing vulgar words.

Each time he scolded me for my hair, I felt a deep sense of anguish and pain inside me. I wanted to cry, to scream, to howl. Whenever I recollect this incident, I get goosebumps all over; I go cold and numb even today.

My other relatives were no less vicious. On a number of occasions, they used me like a prop to ward off negative elements affecting the family. It was a superstitious belief, but malicious enough to upset me.

When a death took place in the family, the elders would dip me in the sea water on amavasya (new moon day) to ward off any negative influences they believed may affect them. They believed that I boded ill luck because I had lost my father as a child. It did not matter which member of the family had passed away; I was called upon to go through all their dim-witted orthodox rites. I was too naïve to be able to see through their malice and innocently went along with their thoughtless rituals. But I felt an acute pain eat at my insides.

I would like to believe that those multiple dips in the sea have washed away my sins and my bad karma. To date, I pay obeisance to the sea as I pass any shore. In Mumbai, I often drive through the coastline at Juhu, Bandra and Marine Drive, and instinctively, I touch my head and rest a hand on my heart as a gesture of gratitude.

Uncle Breaks Wood, Knee

One day, Uncle was chasing me with a baton around the compound until he succeeded in whacking the life out of me. He was grossly offended that I had taken a break for lunch while carrying out one of his never-ending domestic chores. The truth was that it was past 3.00 p.m. and I was famished. He did not seem to be bothered enough to take a break, so I walked away and headed to the kitchen, served myself some food on a plate and had just about squatted on the floor to eat, when he came charging with the stick.

I had been helping him continuously with chopping wood from six in the morning, with only a small interval for breakfast. We were splitting firewood well into noon. He would take breaks for cups of hot tea, while I would get none of it.

I remember that Uncle was partial about food. At lunch, we ate rice, a spicy tomato soup-like concoction called *saaru* and a vegetable. Any plea for a second helping was reciprocated with big eyes reprimanding me, especially during a festival when a sweet dish was part of the preparation. Uncle would relish the meal with large portions, finishing with a bowl of curd and buttermilk. Special menus, such as fish, never found their way to any other family member's plate.

The aforementioned cane-thrashing almost killed my hunger. Uncle, having vented his fury, got back to chopping wood in the backyard, but I suspect his mind was still dithering over my refusal to follow his command.

As I sat in a corner of the house grieving over my pain, I heard a wrenching sound coming from his side. The woodcutting blade had pierced his knee, creating a deep gash in his flesh that began oozing blood. He was badly injured. Unable to balance on one foot, he collapsed on the ground.

For many days thereafter, Uncle was immobile, giving Aunt and me much-needed respite from his violent sprees. In private, Aunt guffawed at his state of pain and helplessness, especially when he moaned in agony in the toilet. The Indian-style toilet bins require one to squat, resulting in the stretching of muscles and bending of bones at the knees, causing excruciating pain. My aunt seemed to derive sadistic pleasure at Uncle's anguish and awkward manner of walking.

'Aiyaiyoo… my legs are no more,' I would hear him cry from the toilet when the wound was fresh. 'What was that (inopportune) time I touched you… aiyaiyoo…,' he moaned endlessly, while Aunt and I chose to keep silent, quietly resuming the work at hand. However, no degree of pain and agony could stop him from accusing me. 'You are responsible for this (hurt),' he would lament at the top of his voice, pointing at me and then at his wound. There was more to come, for in pain or not, Uncle's outrage was a never-ending saga. 'This boy will finish me,' he would repeatedly say, snapping his fingers in the air, muttering vile curses under his breath.

I thought a broken leg would teach him a lesson in humanity. Sadly, I was wrong. Six months after the wound started healing, he was back to his old ways of behaving like a monster in the garb of a human being.

As part of common custom, people tie a thread with lemon and chilli to vehicles to ward off evil. Uncle's idea of a talisman may well have been a rod or a stick kept in every nook and cranny of the house to rid the devils dancing in his evil head. This is how I tried to explain to myself the tyrannical behaviour he unleashed in the name of demanding perfection in my duties.

Burdened with a sore body, scratches, wounds and sometimes, broken bones, I would go to sleep in severe pain on a straw mat with only a simple sheet covering me. Those bruises were never treated. With time, they healed. But the scarred memory remains, even years later.

I cannot forget Uncle's deliberate attempts to hurl insults at me in front of guests. In a brazen display of chauvinism, he would boast that he was the brain behind profitable businesses like the salon, the household milk dairy and the farm.

My aunt too was in the habit of using indecent language in dismissing my work. I wondered if wickedness was a way of life with these people who aped dictatorial feudal lords. It gave them a sense of false supremacy.

I had my first taste of Aunt's viciousness at age seven, when I visited Uncle's place during a school vacation. At the time, they stayed in the salon's tiny backroom that doubled up as a living room and a kitchen in the day, and as a bedroom at night.

One day, in a fit of temper, she caught me and tried to stuff red-hot chillies into my eyes, nose and ears, and into my private parts. She was angry that I had not responded to her call; I was watching a sprinkler watering a neighbourhood plot. The deafening sound of the water engine had muted her voice, but she felt that I had ignored her shouts on purpose.

She dragged me by the neck, a cluster of spicy pods in her fist, determined to punish me. I kept resisting and turning my face left and right, kicking my legs in panic. Somehow, I managed to free myself from her grip and run. Experiencing a maddening burning sensation all over my body and inside my nasal tracts, I tried to cough to clear my throat. The chilly sensation seemed to penetrate my head like a bee sting, sending out a shooting pain.

Running away from her clutches, I squatted under a tree in the compound, crying for help. I developed hives and skin inflammation on my face and the sensitive parts of my body. I was obviously clueless about any cures.

Later, however, my equation with my aunt changed when Uncle's drunken bouts tormented her. He would beat her up too and that was when she began to mellow down towards me. I cannot say she was kind to me, but at least she stopped being malicious. Most times, she was plain indifferent.

But she did alert the household one night, when she found me unconscious with broken teeth and blood oozing out of my mouth. Severely groggy, I had stepped out in the dark to urinate near a bush. My bones were aching after receiving a beating down from Uncle. I stood there worrying about how long I could live a distressed life. I thought of my father—had he been alive, perhaps I would never have been at my relatives' mercy. In that state of depression and slumber, I may have missed a step at the door.

I fell down, breaking three incisors, with cuts on my lips and blood over my face. Aunt heard my cries in the dark. She splashed water and helped me clean the wounds. Much later, while working in Mumbai, I had those broken teeth fixed.

I began to ponder over the reasons that made me comply with Uncle, accompanying him and working under him willingly. I had come with the sole intention of learning haircutting. By now, I was already managing the salon and making visits to people's homes to offer haircuts and shaves. Uncle's dependence on alcohol had worsened over time. It gave me an opportunity to take up responsibility. He preferred to loll in the house all day, thus reducing his work hours at the salon. I had no complaints about taking on the extra workload because it gave me valuable experience in mastering the craft.

But then, I was still being treated brutally, being made a constant victim of his drunken spells. My scars, both physical and mental, were overwhelmingly burdensome. I had become an emotional wreck.

I had already begun mulling over the idea of starting a salon of my own. I thought I could go back to stay with my mother at Attur, as Kariminabai's tenant, where in the village, I could put up a cubicle canopied by coconut branches on the roadside. A stool for my clients and a pair of scissors and a comb was all that I needed to begin. I had this strong urge to become economically independent and stop slaving for Uncle, who absolutely disregarded my efforts.

Then one day, all hell broke loose. I decided I had had enough of Uncle's endless tantrums and his sinister and volatile ways.

That evening, after I returned from the salon, I was in the room, changing from my good pair of shorts into the ones I wore at home. I can say for sure that my uncle was in a sober state, but it appeared that he was in the mood to harass me.

With a mean grin, he started pulling my shorts down and I kept trying to hold back by pulling them up. Then again, he began tugging harder and kept yanking it until he succeeded in removing the clothing completely. The next moment, I was stark naked, a potential victim to ridicule and mockery. Uncle was laughing, enjoying every moment. I was a growing teen and I felt painfully ashamed, standing there like that.

With anger seething inside me, I pushed him away with all my might, grabbed my shorts, wore them and walked away in a huff to show him my obvious disgust. Enraged that I had shown my disapproval to his actions, he let himself loose and began another round of torture.

Grabbing a stick, he began yelling and chasing me around the house. I did my best to escape, but he managed to catch me and thrash me with a bamboo stick (kept at his disposal everywhere in the house). Ruthlessly, he continued hitting me on my back, legs, hands and stomach. To say that I was in acute pain would be an understatement. I controlled my tears and stood there, quietly taking in the beating. I was miserable and in great pain.

Working tirelessly in the hot sun through the day had left me feeling physically drained. I had dug deep trenches on Uncle's orders, to complete thirty such dugouts, to sow coffee saplings. Without a hint of rest during the course of work, I had finished working on fifteen such pits that day, which left my bones aching to the core. To top it all, he hammered the hell out of me.

Then again, wickedly, he ordered me to fetch country liquor from a nearby shop. 'Okay. It's over now. Forget it. Go to the arrack shop.' To what extent can one get evil, I silently wondered.

This time though, I stood my ground. I could not take it anymore. I told him firmly that I would carry out his order if and only if he would let me attend the celebrations of the annual Ganesh Chaturthi festival held at a nearby temple—it was the immersion day of Ganesh idols after ten days of festivities. He was shocked at my demand, but somehow gave in since he needed his alcohol fix.

The plan was to call it quits at Uncle's place so that I could travel back to the place where my mother lived on the pretext of attending the revelry.

I informed my aunt that I was leaving; I even told her that the family should not try to locate me. That night, I left home without speaking to Uncle. I collected some money I had hidden away earlier in the salon and I spent the night sleeping in the shop to board a bus the next morning to Karkala. I met my mother for a brief while. She was happy to see me running away from the clutches of a cruel tyrant. But I was sure that he would not let me be on my own. Hence, I stayed at the house of his in-laws, who knew of his manic ways. It seemed like a safe den.

After two days, my uncle came over to pacify me and to take me away. How did he even expect that I would rejoin him after being tortured all the time? Perhaps he thought I had no option in life, or perhaps he was living in a make-believe world. However, I did not relent. Not one to be swayed by sweet talk and fake promises, I refused to tag along. He never fulfilled his earlier promise of parting with our family share of the property. After a week's stay, I took the bus to Mumbai.

Uncle Passes Away

Circa 16 January 2014. Govind Bhandary passed away. He was seventy-eight years old.

Uncle was suffering from lung cancer for long; he was in extreme pain. I thought he might live longer and everyone else thought so too.

We would speak sometimes over the phone; our last conversation was a week before his death. He was keen to attend the silver jubilee celebration party I had hosted in November 2013, on completion of twenty-five years of my first salon in Mumbai. He wanted a group photo of the family on the occasion; he felt that he was my guru, my teacher.

In his entire lifetime, even on his deathbed, he did not once regret the brutal treatment he had meted out to me.

Aunt too, who was unwell for some time, passed away in early 2019. Their son and daughters are married and settled in life. The salon's shutters are down, the cowshed is empty, and the milk business is no more.

Uncle attended my wife Anushree's *shrimanta*, the baby

shower ritual, held during the seventh month of the first pregnancy, in Mumbai in 2010. He visited me at our apartment. My wife was carrying our son Rohil.

Since he would read about me in the newspapers or see me on television, he expressed a sense of pride at my achievements. He felt elated at my success in the field, but talked about it in a rather backhanded manner. He never praised me directly to my face because he would say that my grounding had come from him. Even in that ailing state, he was full of bluster. Hence, he felt I owed him all credit for my success in the field. I would simply nod my head.

Living with him at that impressionable age taught me to deal with life's vagaries. When I look back in sadness, it feels like a huge aberration in my growing years, but I cannot wipe out that phase of my life. I see that period of my childhood as a kind of learning that no school could ever have taught me.

Every person has faults. If only one realises those errors and corrects them to become a better human being, it is fair to say that one has overcome the mistakes and hurts inflicted upon others. Life's journey must end with a sense of completion. Everyone has to die some day. But at least the last days of one's life should be happy and peaceful.

I am no longer angry with my uncle or aunt. I hold no grudges. If this early phase had never occurred in my life, perhaps I would never have found my calling in life. Nearly four years at Yelemadalu gave direction to my future... They showed me the path to a coiffeur's world.

I can only be thankful.

If you believe in living a respectable life, you believe in self-help, which is the best help.

—*Dr Babasaheb Ambedkar, Father of the Indian Constitution*

chapter five

THE RICH, THE POOR AND THE 'SALOON'

The Mushroom Cut

While the home front in scenic Yelemadalu was a place trapped in Uncle's tyrannical reign, the salon located in a hamlet called Durgadabetta, a few kilometres down the curvy road, was a different world altogether.

In the midst of tropical forests, jagged hills, babbling streams, miles and miles of land carpeted in tea gardens and coffee estates, it was the only haircutting salon for the rich, the poor, the well-to-do and the lowly in Yelemadalu and surrounding villages.

There was no board indicating the name of the barber's shop, but people knew it existed and they called it the 'saloon', drawling out the letter 'o' in their local accent.

I was an apprentice, worker, helper, servant—a combination of all that and more for my uncle, who was the owner of the shop. In short, I was at his beck and call.

It is here that I learnt to use the five-finger blade, a unique implement rarely used or seen these days in a barber's kit. It has a blade fixed with five rings that your fingers can slide into, much like wearing a glove. For a trained barber, once this instrument is firmly in grip, it is one of the best tools to manoeuvre any type of hair.

The device is best suited to give a 'scissor's cut'. This style keeps the hair short at the top portion of the head, tapering the lower side down to the neck, revealing the skin above the nape. An extremely functional crop leaving no scope for dishevelled looks, it always sits elegantly on the person sporting it.

Nowadays, a similar style is popularly known as the 'mushroom cut'. It gets the name due to its close resemblance to the fungus's umbrella-like design. Schoolchildren and college students vie for this cut. In the seventies, this hairdo, also called the 'slope back', was the preferred style among 'writers'—those who managed paperwork in tea gardens and coffee estates.

Writers were suave men in starched khaki shorts, spotless, crisp white shirts and bowler hats that nearly covered the forehead. Swinging a baton in hand, like police officers, their walk evoked awe and admiration among simple village folk. They were academically well qualified too; so in every sense, they were a few notches above ordinary people.

To me, they were reminiscent of the British Raj, simply because of the manner in which they stepped out in heavy rubber gumboots that reached up to their knees. They commanded respect wherever they went.

The first time I used the five-finger blade razor was on one such writer, but only after working the tool several times over my own hair. My uncle insisted that before attending to a customer, I be thorough in my work. For that, I practised the cut on my head several times, just as I practised the shaving blade on my hairy legs and arms before carrying out shaving jobs on clients.

Those were my first lessons in becoming adept at wielding tools with complete confidence. Learning to feel the tool on my skin and hair and trying to understand how it works to avoid injuring clients was part of the training process. It was like homework given to students in school. Working on tools to sharpen my skills was my rehearsal, my homework. When the opportunity presented itself to style a writer's hair, I was more than ready. More than half-a-dozen writers visited the salon every month to trim their hair. They comprised the prestigious category of clients deserving the special treatment reserved for honoured guests.

A writer's visit would signal a flurry of activity in the salon. As the stately man entered, a stony silence would engulf the place and clients would quickly vacate the barber's chair for the man to have his haircut. They would wait outside the salon as the place accommodated only two chairs for clients. A curious crowd would gather at the doorway and peep in, admiring the writer on the seat.

Uncle would by then have made eye contact with me, indicating the order for a quick clean-up of the place. I had to dust and wipe out specks of hair residue stuck to the wooden chair. The indigenous barber's wooden chair had a backrest consisting of a long strip with a handle on top. This handle needed to be pulled to adjust the seat according to the client's height.

Uncle was particular about personally attending to writers. As for me, he thought I was still a novice. It was only after he got addicted to drinking liquor that the charge of running the salon fell on my shoulders. And with that came the responsibility of giving spiffy haircuts to writers as well. By then, I had become quite a professional. Writers always appreciated my effort.

There were others too who graced the respected category of clients.

There was the middle-aged hotelier Kunhiappa—everyone called him Saibera or Saheb—who ran a transport business near our salon. The pot-bellied man, usually attired in a blue-and-white checked lungi and a perforated synthetic vest, carried a small knife called *bisati*, tucked at the waist. He had an intimidating personality and nobody dared to mess around with him.

Although he looked no different from the rest of the Beary Muslim community that he belonged to and the elderly men among them who dressed in a similar fashion, for some reason, Kunhiappa commanded fear as well as respect. I, however, felt he was harmless and a kind soul.

Tall and hefty, sporting a handlebar moustache, Kunhiappa exhibited an amusing habit. Soon after getting his beard and hair trimmed, he would bounce up from the chair as if he had been resting his back on a springboard. Then he would stand raising his hands high in the air! It was like a perfect holdup scene in a thriller movie! It appeared as though someone was holding a gun to his back.

But that was only Kunhiappa's indication to shave his underarms!

Every time this happened, quiet chortles and controlled sniggers would waft in from the shop's doorstep. People waited to see this sight. It was some sort of a joke for the regulars who hung around outside the shop. Obviously, this entire drama took place behind Kunhiappa's back; nobody dared laugh to his face.

Sometimes, I too would feel like chuckling at the comical sight. Of course, I would never do any such thing that might cause embarrassment to our client. I would lower my head, keep a poker face, and quietly carry on with work.

His characteristic gesture was, in fact, a cue for us to take up the next task. As Kunhiappa stood with his hands aloft, I would shave his underarms to clean out the deep sockets of all the messy undergrowth. It was important to him to get rid of underarm hair since he wore a sleeveless vest at all times. Frankly, it was an eyesore, and smelly too. But then, who could complain about hygiene? These were merely occupational hazards.

Then there was Vasu, priest at the local temple and supplier of home-brewed liquor for my uncle. His quaint ears tickled my funny bone to no end. I smiled inwardly while looking at him and was always quick to cover my mouth with my palm, hoping he had not seen me. A bald pate and a long moustache complemented his holier-than-thou persona.

What put him in a distinct category were his hairy earlobes—the hair like miniature Japanese fans on either side with follicular tufts curled out at the rim.

He took immense care to maintain those precious fins, combing them ever so often. Tied to his waist in the folds of his mundu (a white lungi with a traditional border), he kept a tiny comb for the purpose, since he needed to brush them regularly. Besides oiling, washing and trimming the hair on his earlobes, he secretly enjoyed twirling out the black strands with a flourish, unmindful of anyone's presence.

These were some of the special clients who visited the salon regularly.

The Rich

Then there were others, who never visited the salon.

There were prosperous traders, wealthy agriculturists and the village headman, for whom stepping into a haircutting shop was socially demeaning. They needed a barber to provide services at their homes. Every week, or every fortnight, I would make personal visits to shave or trim their beards, while Uncle would cut their hair. That was only for a while; later, I made the visits by myself.

These outings, if I were to describe them in some way, since Uncle would never let me go anywhere outside his watchful orbit, transported me to another world. People at the salon talked in awe about the extravagant lifestyles of the wealthy.

And here I was in close quarters, so close that I had to peer down at the face of the rich to shave and trim their beards and overgrown hair. Indeed, for the bit of work I did, the treatment meted out to me was only kindness. I cannot say that it was the same with workers or farm labourers going there. They moved about in the vicinity with a sense of fear, always anxious to please and were woefully subservient.

I was once trimming a wealthy farmer's hair after doing his beard; I was engrossed in giving it a good outline. As I moved around his head, clipping unwanted bits of hair, his head resting at an angle on the reclining chair, I noticed that his eyes appeared to be looking at the coconut palm leaves swaying against the clear blue sky and his thoughts were perhaps somewhere in the wilderness.

He appeared unmindful of the poor peasant kneeling down a few yards away, looking utterly helpless. 'Please don't beat me. I am unwell,' came the quivering voice of the worker from a distance. 'Dhani... I am running a high fever, my body is aching...'

The rich farmer, addressed as Dhani, a local designate for a property owner, was an autocrat to workers, who felt subjugated working under him. In the interior parts of tea estates, I had seen, from a distance during my daily errands, the farmer's underlings mercilessly beating up workers when they appeared to be going against their master's wishes.

Workers were whipped ruthlessly—their agonising cries travelled far in the thick of trees, leaves and shrubbery, merging with the spicy odours of cardamom and pepper, drifting through clusters of fresh green and red coffee beans. But nobody attempted to help them.

Scared of the torture that many others were put through, this peasant was begging for respite. His body was palpably shivering as he was pleading for mercy.

From the corner of my eye, I tried to look at him. I could not, however, as the poor peasant had bent his body low as a mark of respect. What did catch my eyes were ribs protruding out of a thin, bare-chested frame of skin and bones. His skin looked wrinkled and parched like an unwashed, crinkled, coarse cotton cloth. I could imagine that he may not have eaten a morsel for days together.

'What kind of people are these?' I thought to myself quietly, as I usually did when I felt a strong urge to say something. What was in my mind remained entrenched within; I could not risk my thoughts tumbling out of my head.

'Umm…' grunted the wealthy farmer in response, voicing authority in a gruff tone. A monosyllabic reaction heightened the tension even more on that chilly winter day, revealing a pronounced equation between a feudal master and his insignificant servant.

Closing his eyes halfway like he was falling asleep, the wealthy man glanced sideways at his supervisor, as if to seek his opinion. The supervisor, standing closer to his master in a slightly hunched position, head bowed and clutching files to his chest, returned a rather submissive look of waiting to follow the orders of His Highness. He knew that his opinion did not really matter, that his participation was only called for in a feudal mime charade. He went with the flow.

The supervisor was a petty lord unto himself for the area he monitored, and like him, there were many such small lords for groups of peasants working under them. They yelled profanities at workers and generally exhibited cruel behaviour. It was never straight or simple talk.

Dhani raised his hand in the air as if to dust dirt off his fingers. It was a signal for the peasant to go away, a nonchalant indication of permission granted to take the much-needed break.

Thanking him profusely, the poor man folded his hands in

gratitude, like he was worshipping a celestial being descended from heaven, and touched his head to the ground several times over.

Meanwhile, I was done with my task, filled with a pervading sense of relief. The feeling came from having done my work satisfactorily and at seeing the workers' plight mitigated in some way. He could rest for a day. That was a relief.

The peasant feared losing his job at the slightest of personal requests. He was not a local, but a migrant like many others who had fled from famine and drought, along with their families, to escape hunger and death.

In the early seventies, when the monsoons did not spell a drop of rain, farms were dry and parched in the villages of Karnataka, particularly the towns and surrounding areas of Chitradurga, Shimoga and Hasan. Without any source of water, the land became arid and cracked, thrashing all hopes of cultivation.

In coffee estates, despite deprivation and torture, a peasant working on daily wages was sure of feeding his wife and children a few morsels of food. It was definitely not a good situation to be in, but in those circumstances, anything was better than staying hungry.

I knew well enough what hunger pangs felt like. The agony of an empty growling stomach, the pain of going to bed hungry on many nights, even as a child, I could never forget. I empathised with all peasants.

I had set out early from home without my regular morning glass of coffee. The chilly weather was biting at my tummy. A simple woollen muffler was all I had as warm clothing with which I wrapped my ears, protecting them from the cold wind. I craved for hot filter coffee and for a breakfast of steaming idli and sambar. I had to wait, though, until I had finished all my work.

After the family patriarch, the rest of the family members

such as elders, brothers, sons, their children and grandchildren, were in queue. The visit would usually involve servicing an entire family. A long ritual of haircutting went on all through the morning in the sprawling backyard of the heritage structure that the family lived in.

Babies were last in the pecking order. Large families always had a tiny tot or two. Babbling toddlers sat on a wooden plank temporarily fitted on the handles of the wooden chair so that the child reached the eye-level of the barber. Some shrieked when they looked at a pair of scissors and stretched out their tender limbs in refusal. As the act of resistance continued in the form of loud yelping and crying, a family elder would wind his arms from the back around the child, holding the child until the job was through.

The family grooming session took all morning amidst good cheer and banter. It ended in a bathing ritual in the open backyard where water boiled in massive copper pots on firewood. Water remained hot as long as the embers burned. For some reason, after my routine was done, I felt the chill even more. Seeking warmth, I would crawl my way closer to the fire, tugging at my shirt collar with both my hands to fight the cold. I had to wait for my master's orders to take leave.

The rich had their own ways of dealing with the rest of the world. All affluent families invited us for the job at their bidding. An Ambassador car or a jeep would come to our house to fetch us as well as to drop us back after work, as the place would be miles and miles away from our home.

Typically, our payment was an annual lump sum, not given in cash but as a disbursement of rice, millet or any other produce from their farms. They paid us in the form of *mudi*, a casket made out of hay and tied with rope, carrying nearly thirty-eight kilograms of rice grain, our staple food.

One by one, everyone took turns to bathe while the master

of the house, the patriarch, would head to the bathing room located in the yard, but outside the periphery of the home. That was his privilege; he did not partake in the public bathing exercise and neither did he laugh or crack jokes. He usually kept a stern face.

The bathing ritual in the backyard was significant, as nobody entered the inner portals until they had scrubbed and cleaned, pouring copious amounts of water on their bodies. A peculiar custom among Hindus—no family member could touch them until they were, in a sense, purified.

This was the only time one felt like an outcaste. It was a reminder of my low social status, of being born into a family of barbers. It left me feeling disconcerted. It made me wonder if visiting a barber's shop amounted to attending the last rites of the dead at the cremation ground. People bathed on their return before resuming the day's work. Was purification necessary before re-entering the house? These thoughts troubled me as I headed home even though I was driven back in one of their plush cars.

The Poor

The rich and the poor lived in two unusual worlds, diametrically opposite.

While the wealthy were pampered by getting their whims and fancies of grooming catered to within the periphery of their heritage bungalows, the poorest of the poor, being on the other end of the social spectrum, found succour at the salon. It became a place of leisure, bustling with activity.

The salon was located on the outskirts on a relatively quiet road that connected paddy fields, tea plantations, grape-like fresh pepper spice bunches and tiny cardamom pods hanging like little bells on plants grown at the foothills of this picturesque town.

The long winding road facing the shop was lined with a row of casuarinas, their spiked needle-like branches swaying gently in the direction of the wind. Lately, these trees can be seen on top of the hills while the road below is lined with periwinkle flowers and mayflower trees.

On the side of the shop were a couple of eateries, tea stalls, a grocery shop, and a room leased to a schoolteacher, all lined in a row. While across the road were other landmarks of the village—a hotel, a wholesale grocery shop, a municipality office, a post office and a bus stop from where the villagers boarded public transport. All manner of vehicles such as buses, jeeps, motorbikes, lorries and even tractors stopped here to pick up passengers who wanted to travel to nearby towns. The mention of these amenities may make it seem like it were a self-sufficient community; nevertheless, it was a tiny village.

Travellers, tourists, visitors, traders, buyers, elders, youngsters, children and everyone else who turned up in the above places invariably dropped by at the salon. It became a favourite haunt of locals, workers and peasants who whiled away their time there, soaking in the leisurely atmosphere if they had nothing better to do in the village. There was much to talk and gossip about.

In the midst of greenery, the tiny barber's shop was a world in itself, with a series of goings-on enveloping it. The fifty-five-square foot shop's tin sheet cover, placed precariously on brick walls, had a worn-out exterior and a swinging door. When a client pushed it open and walked in, the door behind him would jangle a bit back and forth and then shut by itself. Inside, the furniture was a bare minimum.

There were two wooden chairs, long headrests, a wooden table and two small mirrors that hung on a wall replete with patches of peeling paint. The table spread with the barber's paraphernalia, which consisted of an elongated bottle of plain water fitted with a spray, some combs, a couple of scissors and body soap from the well-known Godrej company; being slightly overpriced compared to other bath soaps, it was considered to be of a superior class.

Shaving creams were a luxury those days; besides they were not available, not in the village, not even in nearby towns, but only in faraway Madras (now Chennai) city in the neighbouring state. The soap, costing not less than twenty-five paise, then called four annas, was a convenient substitute for a shaving cream because it could form lather.

An assorted range of glitzy pictures torn out of magazines camouflaged cracks and damp spots on the shop's walls. These pictures belonged to film stars of Kannada movies and top cricketers of the time who played for the country. Cricketers were everybody's heroes, but the pictures plastered on the walls were of Gundappa Vishwanath, Chandrashekar, Prassanna, Brajesh Patel and Roger Binny, because they all hailed from Karnataka.

During test matches, the radio blared, as a motley crowd camped through the day, listening to the five-day game commentary. Applauding at every four and six, they would deliberate over each shot and ball. The humble transistor brought all news, information, songs and entertainment to our houses and shops, unimaginable now in the days of twenty-four-hour television and the internet airing live telecasts of the T20 format. Even one-day matches seem ancient now.

The damp walls had other pictures too. Actors posing with a bouffant and hair loosely falling on the forehead were a visual treat for clients, who liked to ogle at cherry lips and painted faces. International tennis players looking wet and sweaty after playing a hard game left all of us in awe. Subconsciously, this is where I began nursing a desire to play the game. Later, while working in a club in Qatar, I learnt to pick up the racket and took to the sport, which I play to date.

The biggest eye-candy was the late M.G. Ramachandran, popular as MGR and the most-admired icon of Tamil films in the seventies. He enjoyed a god-like status, so a life-size effigy of the actor-turned-politician adorned the entrance of the shop. Many travellers from Madras often visited the salon, hence Uncle thought that a poster showing the star in colourful clothes would please the actor's fans. Later, MGR became a prominent politician in the south and the chief minister of Tamil Nadu, with an even bigger following.

Uncle imagined himself to be quite the swashbuckling hero who wore a bouffant hairdo with thick sideburns. He aped his screen idol down to the last detail, sporting an extravagant puff of hair, wearing khaki shorts, a banian and a Madras check shirt. He detested wearing a lungi, for only rural folk wore that attire.

Our largest clientele were scruffy, dirty and unkempt peasants working in coffee estates. They were simple labourers who toiled all day under the blistering sun. Trudging barefoot into the shop with muck on their sweaty, hairy chests, they came to us for a haircut.

It would be a weekly holiday, either a Sunday or Saturday—the only time they bathed in the week—when their cleaning routine began at our shop by first doing away with unwanted hair. They opted for a crew cut or a plain short trim to avoid the hassle of combing every day.

I doubted if they ever held a mirror to their face in their homes. The only time they did so was probably when we gave them a haircut. We would hold a small mirror behind their head for them to be able to get a view of the short crop. If we said it was fine, then it was definitely good for them. My uncle's knowledge of hairstyles was limited to the demands made by people visiting the salon. Besides, village people were simple folk who had no inkling of grooming, unlike their fashion-conscious urban counterparts. Any haircut we gave them would be appreciated.

Many other locals were far more messy. They did not practise even the basic habit of keeping their hair clean. As a result, we would have smelly, unwashed hair carrying lice, dandruff and festering boils and infection on our hands. But their unclean living patterns did not matter; our duty was to do our job.

Perhaps the most unkempt of the lot would be the foul-smelling nomads making annual pilgrimage visits. The womenfolk clothed in myriad colours, embroidery, sparkling mirrors, jewellery and trinkets lent the much-needed spectacle to our quiet leafy locale. They had peculiar hairdos with old coins tied to their hair that hung down till their cheekbones, covering most of the face. All that fancy headgear must have been cumbersome and would have tugged down heavily on the hair, yet they did not seem to mind. For them it was part of their normal dress. But they were completely lacking in their sense of cleanliness.

Men and women looking hardy, with many children in tow, would alight from tractors in droves and squat in front of the shop or by the roadside with their luggage. They did not carry bags as luggage, but huge cloth bundles stuffed with clothes and other belongings. Boys aged between three and four years crouched, as Uncle and I randomly cut off their matted hair. It would be the first haircut of their lives as I always suspected that they never ever washed their hair. The stinking dreadlocks were then taken away to offer in temples in the area as part of a traditional ritual.

To me, they were by far the most unhygienic people who camped in the area for a long time. By day, they took up work at construction sites and by night, they were sloshed in country liquor, men and women alike, sleeping by the edge of the road, oblivious to their surroundings. Being the poorest of the poor, for them, haircuts were free.

Our dreams have to be bigger. Our ambitions higher. Our commitments deeper. And our efforts greater.

—Dhirubhai Ambani, business visionary and founder of Reliance Industries

chapter six

DOGS, GLITTERING LIGHTS AND THE SKYSCRAPERS OF MUMBAI

I woke up from deep slumber onboard a bus to Mumbai. Dreamily, I looked out of the window into the twilight sky streaked in orange and mauve against the setting sun. Another day was ending as the evening gradually melted into night, setting the skyline aglow with a sea of lights.

We were passing some town. I did not know the name and it did not matter. I was happy and excited that I was travelling to the city of dreams. It was the joy of freedom, of being free from the chains of bondage, away from the tyranny of my uncle. Finally, I could be on my own.

Mumbai, in my imagination, as the relatives with whom I was travelling narrated, was a city of glittering lights, tall buildings, fancy cars and affluent people. Everyone flocked to the moneyed city to become rich. I too hoped to become prosperous someday.

Still sleepy, I turned to look around inside the bus and noticed a fellow traveller seated beside me. A saintly looking elderly man wearing a faded ochre stole and a white tunic smiled benignly and started talking to me. There was something appealing about him; the stubble and grey hair exuded an aura of maturity and from his eyes emanated a sense of calm. He radiated a magnetic personality.

Talking gently in soft and measured tones, he had a mesmerising effect on me. In my life, this far, I felt that nobody had spoken to me so kindly as this saintly person.

He enquired about my cousin Vasanthi and her husband Vithal Bhandary, who were occupying the seats in front of me. They had offered to help me find a job at one of the many salons run by their relatives in Mumbai; however, they could not promise that I would land with one immediately.

But that was enough for me. I carried along a new pair of trousers and a shirt, which I had recently got sewn, and some money taken from the savings stashed away in the salon niche. I even paid about ₹35 for my travel ticket for the journey of nearly two days and a night.

The benign elder asked me if I was travelling to Mumbai for the first time.

'Mumbai exemplifies two categories. There is hell, and there is heaven,' he thoughtfully explained. 'One day you can become a millionaire and the next day you may become bankrupt…' he continued.

I listened to him intently. He outlined the socio-economic landscape of the city, saying there were people residing in the metropolis belonging to various communities, including prosperous Gujaratis and Marwaris. Elaborating on their businesses, faiths, their struggle to survive, he described that the shrine of Goddess Mumbadevi protected the city.

All this information that he was conveying was new to me. I got the feeling that he was preparing me to be vigilant in a big city beset with a multitude of contradictions.

'Do not go where there are crowds. Stay away from mobs. In case you see people watching a street fight, don't join them or become part of the group. Such fights take place often. Don't even try to find out what is going on there; you might be dragged into a messy fracas for no fault of yours…'

In a twenty-minute talk, he advised me to be careful with my money. 'Save it. Do not spend. You have to take care.'

I listened to him carefully, trying to assimilate his words of caution. However, there was one thing that troubled me a lot. I waited for a while, and then I thought I must ask him.

'Are there dogs in Mumbai?' I enquired gingerly, my gullibility laid bare.

My question could have surprised anybody, but not him, he was unfazed. He simply smiled back. Perhaps my innocence intrigued him.

It may seem weird, but of all the worries in the world, in a metropolis where people's concerns were about making money or making ends meet, I was most anxious about dogs biting me!

The reason behind this fear was that in the past, I had been bitten by dogs in the village several times. I could never forget the agony of taking painful injections at the town's government hospital. To top it all, I had to pay for the medication from my meagre savings. Maybe I was worried about bearing needless hospital expenses in an unknown city. Besides, my mother too was not with me. I derived emotional support from her presence.

The fact is that I could not entirely comprehend the sound advice that this saintly person was giving me, although I could sense that he meant well. Years later, as I recollect his words in solitude, I am able to understand its profound essence. The picture of an aged, genteel person still plays in my mind. Looking back, I think our meeting was some sort of divine intervention, guiding me and cautioning me about the future.

Indeed, his advice was a godsend for a young lad brimming with hope and energy to make it big in life. That day though, following our chat, I dozed off. I woke up after an hour or so to find the seat beside me empty. My fellow traveller had disappeared just as suddenly as he had appeared.

I looked out of the bus window to see some more towns and

cities passing by. The panoramic view at dusk was breathtaking, with a carpet of lights stretching far into the horizon. I could see thousands of lights gleaming for miles on end, merging with the stars twinkling across the shining sky. I felt as if those tiny blinking lights were small glimmers of hope around me. It was magical. Enchanted by the sheer luminosity in the darkness outside the glass window, I felt like I was floating in Fairyland.

The excitement of watching Mumbai's bedecked skyline in the night, shining like an ocean of lights, is mind-blowing.

I now stay on the thirty-sixth storey of a towering building in a Mumbai suburb, Oshiwara. At night, as I lie on my bed, from the window I can see the city's tall buildings illuminating innumerable specks of light, some coming out of plush apartments and some from not-so-well-off homes. From a distance, all the lights look the same. The struggle for survival is everyone's battle. Only our dreams and objectives differ. Further up, the sky gleams with twinkling stars. Cushioned in the midst of blinking lights, my heart skips a beat and I feel like a child once again. I want to jump. I want to clap. It brings immense joy to my heart. Even now, I like to peep out of the window during night landings when my flight touches the low skyline. I opt for a window seat to look at the million lights glowing on the ground below… glittering jewels reflecting Mumbai's lustre.

Going back to my journey… On reaching Mumbai, I was a bit awestruck by the milling crowds. They reminded me of ants moving in a straight row, without looking left or right. While working in my uncle's garden, I would often watch ants crawling in slow motion, one behind another. Their sense of direction and order was fascinating. Looking down from the bus's window at the swarming heads moving on course brought back memories. They were quite like those ants, rushing and speeding to work.

Pollution was looming thick in the air, the humidity was unbearable and the air smelled fetid. Villages, in comparison, were clean and fresh in the morning. However, weather conditions were no deterrent. I had to find work.

Getting a job in Mumbai was not an easy task, I figured, as I toured the vicinity of Bhandup, where I had put up with Vithal. He was a simple man, and still is so, besides being a kind soul and helpful by nature. During one of our visits, he pointed to a tall building, indicating a shop in the arcade that belonged to his family. In my naiveté, I misunderstood that they owned the entire multi-storeyed building.

I was impressed with my relatives' achievements. I wondered if I could ever do anything like that. My mind was buzzing with doubts about my ability to succeed and to acquire name and fame in my field. Then I thought, why not? I could put in as much effort and hard work as my cousins did, and I would be able to manage on my own.

This was a pivotal turning point in my life. The multi-storeyed building I stood looking at sent my ambitions soaring.

The dreams of owning several salons with a huge client base were big. But then, did I even know how to operate a blow-dryer? It was essential to have that basic knowledge since clients in Mumbai, unlike village folk, were fussy about getting their hair set after a cut. I was building castles in the air.

My first job was at a small salon called Ajanta, run by Vithal's cousin Anand Bhandary. It was located in Khindipada, Bhandup West, a dangerous place, known for killings and illegal activities. A client, who was in a hurry to get his hair set, forced me to use the gadget, explaining how to operate the system. Anand, the only one who operated the fancy electronic device, was not in the shop. I thought this was the moment to learn.

Imagine my excitement when I held the electronic dryer for the first time in my life. I was fumbling, but extremely excited.

My joy knew no bounds. It was a tiny appliance, unlike the large ones used in salons nowadays. I faltered a bit, but the client who was in a mad rush hardly cared. He ordered me to use it immediately to dry and set his hair.

Thereafter, I began using the dryer regularly like a professional, mainly for clients keen to have a haircut like Bollywood movie stars. It was the early eighties, when everyone wanted hair like the dancing sensation Mithun Chakraborty and sideburns like superstar Amitabh Bhachchan.

Anand was a kind-hearted soul; he was like a window through which I could peep into a world beyond my work. He was my guide, patiently teaching me to board local trains from Kanjurmarg station, located close to the salon. Since I was not yet a regular commuter, I nearly lost my way a few times.

One day, while trying to board a packed train from Dadar, in central Mumbai, to Kanjurmarg, near Bhandup, towards north-east Mumbai, I was left hanging at the doorstep, clutching the window at the side of the train with one hand. Like all newcomers to the city, I found directions confusing. I did not realise that the train was an outstation one and not a local. This meant that it was heading out of Mumbai!

I realised my folly when the train whizzed past several local stations with me hanging, holding on for dear life. Scared out of my wits, I felt dizzy—the speeding train felt like a flash of lightning blazing through a dark tunnel. A tape recorder, the purchase I had made at Dadar for my relatives, was strapped across my shoulder. My vision blurred, with the swift breeze hitting my face full-force. Somehow I could detect electric poles ahead on the side of the track, and was able to evade them by pushing my way in. Much later, when the train stopped at Kalyan Junction, on the outskirts of the city, I scampered onto the next platform to board a local back home. After this unpleasant incident, I was particularly careful while getting into trains.

I tasted the bitterness of beer for the first time when Anand took me to a shady liquor bar one day. We shared a glass with potato chips and peanuts. I wondered what made people gloat about drinking something that smelt stale and tasted acrid. I enjoyed the accompanying snacks though. My initiation into North Indian cuisine such as roti, tandoori chicken sukha (dry) and food seasoned with garam masala was thanks to Anand, who took me to restaurants and introduced me to Punjabi fare. He also let me use the space in his shop to sleep at night. The area, however, was known for its notoriety. Each week, we heard of at least three murders and the police would find the abandoned bodies on a vacant land in the vicinity. Terrified, nobody ventured out in the middle of the night. We too firmly shut the shop's doors.

I worked here for about fifty days for a salary of ₹45 per month, and saved a bit from clients' tips. Anand was pleased at my keenness to attend to every client and my efforts at doubling working hours on Sundays. It was a temporary job as, soon after, Vithal shifted me to another salon belonging to his younger brother Raghu, in Bhandup.

Raghu's nature was quite the opposite of Vithal's. A self-made man, Raghu stayed reserved, not bothering about the world outside his workspace. Since he was a habitual miser, he could never help anyone in adversity.

Those traits did not bother me. I needed a job and Raghu's salon was big. It could accommodate four customers at a time, hence there was scope for more work. I faced a problem initially as clients who were familiar with regular barbers chose to get their hair done by them. I would wait at hand and watch them work.

I decided to utilise this time productively by observing my colleagues wield their scissors and I learnt new haircuts as they styled clients. I tried to cultivate cordial relations with clients who awaited their turn to get a haircut. I would approach them with magazines to read or offer to fetch them drinking water. Most of them were mill workers and labourers working in surrounding industrial units.

If a client was bored or yawned, I would rush out to get a cutting chai or tea from a nearby pavement stall. 'Cutting chai' is the local name, popular in Mumbai, for half a cup of tea; in this case, it was a small glass. I shared a comfort level with customers hailing from Mangalore, and from Kerala and Tamil Nadu. I often attempted to build stronger bonds by speaking with them in their mother tongue.

It took several months for me to become a full-time barber. It was only after Mohan, a colleague, quit his job that I got the opportunity to be one.

The focus of my life was just one thing—my work. The salon was the only place I spent all my waking hours, catering to clients and drawing a salary of ₹60 per month, in addition to a five percent commission. I spent the nights on the verandah of a nearby school or in the premises of a local temple. During the rains, the loft of Raghu's one-room house, located in the backyard of the salon where he lived with his wife and son, served the purpose. I hesitatingly asked Raghu if I could use the shop to sleep in the monsoon, but he admonished me by saying, 'Who will pay the electricity bills?'

After working for two-and-a-half years, Raghu entrusted me with the shop's responsibility, including managing accounts, since he moved to Saudi Arabia to work for a short period.

Living in Bhandup was one of the toughest phases of my life. Close to the salon was a fairly large slum overrun by thugs and petty pickpockets, and a den where adulterated liquor was manufactured. A man once tried to pull my wallet from the back pocket of my trousers as I was walking in the teeming market yard. As a precautionary measure, I stood there, waited and avoided turning around when I sensed a hand resting on the wallet. In a while, I heard something fall down.

Then I turned around, and the man behind me quickly pointed to the wallet on the ground. Both of us bent to pick it up from the road. All along we were pretending as though nothing was wrong. As soon as I collected my wallet, the man disappeared in the crowd. That is the closest I have come to facing a thief's wiliness.

Thugs were known to move with knives and other sharp objects hidden inside their shirts. I witnessed rioters on the streets, charging at people with swords, when Bhiwandi's communal riots in the early eighties spilled over into our area. Those were troubled times. One community was pitted against the other, thirsting for blood. One day, pushing the front wooden four-flap door open, a man came charging into our salon to take away the barber's razor blade. He wanted to use it as a weapon to kill. I looked at his face; his bloodshot eyes were raging with anger. I tried to pacify the angry-looking man, who, incidentally, was our client, explaining that in Raghu's absence, the responsibility of taking care of the shop rested on me.

'Please don't do this,' I pleaded. 'If something goes wrong, I will be blamed.' He kept venting his fury because he wanted to get back at some people. I was frightened out of my wits. 'Please, sir, do not do anything that will land me in trouble,' I begged.

It took a lot of convincing, but he finally calmed down. He went away without taking the sharp blade, but left huffing and puffing, all the time muttering abuses under his breath. Outside, the air was putrid, emitting stench and smoke everywhere. People were burning rubber tyres, running with sticks and batons and randomly pelting stones at houses. Most of all, for the first time in my life, I saw fear on people's faces, the terror of an unknown enemy. Everyone was afraid that somebody would come to kill them. Nobody was safe, and that included me. After all those days in Mumbai, I felt like an outsider and I wanted to escape. But I realised that I now shouldered a bigger responsibility—that of safeguarding Raghu's shop. Until tensions eased out, I had to stay put. That period was like a nightmare I can never forget.

For nine months, I looked after Raghu's shop as if it were my own. I personally took care of everything, including washing salon towels and cleaning the place. My only entertainment at the time was watching kabaddi games held at the local gymnasium grounds in Maharashtra Nagar. Big teams of young boys representing various suburbs in the city competed with each other, drawing huge crowds.

The games were immensely thrilling and the ground was always charged with excitement. Since there was no seating facility, the crowd was on its feet, huddled together and pushing one another to seek a vantage point. My short height (I was still growing at age fifteen) was a disadvantage. I had to crane my neck to catch a few glimpses.

I decided to squat on my haunches to peer through the gaps between people's legs. There were scrawny limbs, fat ones, some tall and others puny, covered in flared trousers or bell-bottoms, fashionable in the seventies. Each time a leg moved, my view was obstructed, compelling me to shift my gaze. I moved to the right and then to the left—it was like watching a movie in a makeshift tent, the ones in villages where poles and stilts in the auditorium block the scene.

After twisting and turning my back and neck and trying out different positions, I would manage to grab a bit of the scuffle on the dusty ground as one team pulled the opposing team member's leg to evict him from the game. Both teams would try to outdo the other by running across the opposing team's territory to win over. It was quite a task to watch the entire game, but I enjoyed it immensely.

One night, as the match was on and I was peeping between a pair of bell-bottoms, an elderly person bent down and remarked smilingly in Marathi, the language I was beginning to grasp.

'Ghuus, baala, ghuus,' meaning 'Push in, child, push in,' and he thrust me forward to let me crawl ahead. Taken in by his enthusiasm, I started moving slowly ahead in the maze of legs, feet, shoes and slippers until I reached the front row. The crowd, busy cheering, whistling and hooting, was oblivious to a small creature on all fours sneaking his way in. I joined in the euphoria. I cannot even explain how delighted I was watching the game. And to think of the efforts I made to view the match from the front row is even more hilarious.

Later, I had to quit the job following constant cribbing and misunderstandings with Raghu's wife. After an ugly fracas, I departed to go home to my mother in Karkala. However, in less than a week, I returned to work at another cousin's shop.

This time, while I was travelling to Mumbai, I nearly died when the bus met with an accident, sliding ten feet down a cliff, killing the woman sitting behind me. I recall exiting the vehicle, stuck at an odd angle in mud and rocks, from the front glass cover of the driver's cabin!

Clutching my red suitcase (the colour helped me locate my luggage instantly in the chaos) with its broken handle, I trekked up the hill and hitched a ride in another bus heading to Mumbai. The ghastly accident had left me feeling devastated. On reaching Mumbai, the normalcy among people going about their everyday work helped me gather my frayed nerves. I was back in a regular environment, feeling secure and grateful for being saved.

In the sprawling slum area of Ramabai Nagar, Ghatkopar East, I found my new dwelling. And with that, I became one of the hundreds and thousands who seek shelter under tin sheets, with overflowing open gutters and garbage mounds on the side for company. The stench was overpowering. One had to learn to live in the midst of dirt and filth. Mosquitoes looked like monsters, so big that ten such mosquitoes, I imagined, could lift a person up into the air! Infections spread via mosquitoes frightened me. Anything remotely connected with doctors and hospitals was enough to scare me.

The hutment belonged to Vithal's cousin, coincidentally also called Anand Bhandary, and his wife Rukmini, and was sandwiched in a row of huts. At the Ramabai Nagar slum, neighbours lived within earshot of each other, and everyone knew what was happening around. It was chaotic and noisy. People shouting, neighbours screaming and early morning quarrels at the municipal water pipe connection by the wayside were a common sight. Residents queued to fill water in pots and buckets for drinking and bathing purposes.

It was a strange place, though. We would bathe in the open, beside mounds of rotting garbage and open gutters so that the soap water flowed into the sewage. Bathing in such an environment, how could you consider yourself clean? Reeking of an obnoxious odour was a hooch-brewing section behind our place. I cannot say which among them was more harmful and unbearable to my olfactory nerves. But I was in no position to complain.

Back home in the village, even though people live in small houses, they are particularly aware of cleanliness. Poor people plaster house floors with cow dung, considered an organic disinfectant, because they cannot afford to lay tiles. In the absence of tarred roads, alleyways are covered with cobblestones. A certain standard of hygiene is adhered to. One will never find mounds of trash piled on the roadside.

Soon, a work offer came up in Dharavi, an area once reputed

to be Asia's biggest slum pocket. I refused the job outright after visiting the salon as it was located in front of a beef shop. Long masses of red meat of slaughtered cattle hung down from hooks and repulsed me instantly. My mind was not willing to take up the work despite being jobless. For a large part of my growing up years, I lived with cattle, milking, grazing and feeding them. To see them being hacked in front of my eyes was unacceptable. The surroundings were disturbing and I felt nauseated.

Fourteen days later, my job search ended when Anand put me up in another distant cousin's salon called 'Alankar', located in the buzzing Gandhi market in Ghatkopar. The advantage of working here was that I could sleep in the shop. My meals were at small eateries. Bathing in the open had become a habit. Most times, I wore damp shorts since my clothes never dried after washing. I lay them down to dry inside the salon at night after closing the shop.

For a few months, I dabbled in two jobs. In the day, I worked at a salon and late in the night, I sold lemonade on a roadside cart along with my cousin, Krishna, who had come to Mumbai for a job. Krishna was my childhood playmate and as teenagers, we had shared beedis (a cheap and heady version of a cigarette, containing unfiltered tobacco rolled in a leaf), secretly puffing, away from the prying eyes of elders. We rented a cart for ₹10 per day, purchased a steel vessel, drum and a spoon, and profitably sold the refreshing drink during the nine-day festival of Navratri at the Gandhi Market circle. After a fortnight, we graduated to selling dosas, chutney and sambar.

I started making small savings from the extra money I earned. My first pair of sneakers was a used product purchased from a pavement cobbler selling second-hand sports shoes. The footwear's snug fit and white colour was just what I was looking for. It gave me a tremendous feeling of comfort and instilled in me a sense of authority. In the village, people believed that only top officers wore boots. I was excited with my new purchase costing ₹15, a fairly large amount, especially when I had to dig into my savings to afford it.

In my heart, I thanked the man who had given away or sold the pair to this cobbler. I wondered whose shoes I was slipping my feet into. He may have been a prosperous man who left a good pair behind. I considered myself lucky to be wearing a blessed soul's footwear.

Business at the salon progressed in leaps and bounds, forcing us to stretch our working hours to midnight. I could barely help Krishna in his food stall, owing to the extra time I needed to put in at the salon. I swapped my work with a cousin, Shivanna Bhandary, a simpleton from the village, who was badly in need of a job. Our business was short-lived, though. One night, the cart slipped out of Shivanna's grip on a sloping road, slid down and banged into a parked car, breaking its glass windows. After paying off the damages, we had to shut shop.

Meanwhile, the endless stream of clients helped me learn the nitty-gritties of salon business as Alankar started reaping profits. However, Raghu's arrival from Saudi Arabia put a spanner in the works. He dragged me back to his salon, assuring me that his wife would not bother me again. I had respect for Raghu; it was his wife I found to be nasty. I joined back to assist him in his salon.

Every incident in my life has been a great source of learning, literally educating me in what I perhaps missed out on in a formal school education. I may not know lessons from the books of say, history or geography, but numerous challenges have prepared me to deal with practical issues.

At Raghu's salon, because of the varied clientele, it gave me an opportunity to brush up my knowledge of languages such as Tamil, Malayalam and Konkani spoken in the style and dialect of natives in Mangalore. I am well-versed in what is popularly known as the Mangalore Beary bhasha, a mix of several south Indian languages, spoken by the Muslim community in and around Mangalore.

Tulu and Kannada were the languages spoken at home, the latter being the medium of my education until Class Five. Therefore, I am able to read and write. I was also fond of reading booklets that published devotional songs and translating them into Tulu.

At the salon, I learnt Hindi, Marathi and Gujarati, spoken locally. Since a large number of customers spoke these languages, my interactions helped me learn how to converse in them. This knowledge has taken me a long way in my business by enabling me to fluently communicate with clients.

After working in Qatar, with my experiences that I will write more about in the following chapter, I learnt to speak Arabic in the Doha-Qatar dialect. Along the way, I picked up spoken English as well.

Initially, I went through *Rapidex*, a guidebook for learning languages, to translate Kannada words into English. I began to decipher film advertisements depicting pictures in newspapers. I read the well-known Marathi newspaper *Maharashtra Times*, available at the salon, to identify vernacular syllables and words; some were more or less similar to Hindi. I would compare identical movie advertisements appearing in Kannada and Marathi newspapers with the English film weekly *Screen*, to be able to learn the same word in three different languages.

My efforts at learning languages sound a bit complicated, but in reality, it was a simple exercise. When in doubt, I would not hesitate to ask customers or people at the salon for the correct pronunciation and meaning. People were more than eager to resolve my confusion. Now I am pretty comfortable reading in Hindi and English, although writing down words is still a challenge.

I believe, when one makes an effort to learn, the mind automatically helps one understand and leads one to answers. My mid-teens were an impressionable age when I was open to learning, making mistakes and re-learning lessons from everyone around me. Watching people conduct themselves taught me about human nature and behavioural patterns. To imbibe rather than react to actions helped me to understand and deal with people.

Raghu's wife Chandravati cooked food for us in a kitchen behind the salon. But she was a personification of negativity. Several times, we would be locked in a war of words. She would keep our food plates on a small window sill in the wall dividing the salon and the kitchen in the adjoining room.

If I was busy attending to a client and late at picking up my plate, I would find flies and mosquitoes swimming or dead in the dal and rice. It never occurred to her to top the plate with a cover to ward off insects. I thought it was a deliberate attempt to spurn me.

Raghu would try to intervene to sort out our disputes. He was keen to have me there since I worked all days in the week, including Monday, the salon's weekly holiday. It helped to increase business to about ₹50-80 per day, which was a lot for a small salon that charged just about ₹7 for a haircut. Despite many differences with his wife, I continued to work there since Raghu would part with nearly fifty percent of the commission for Monday's work.

My mother's wish was that I should work in the Middle East, just like many village people who had flown out and changed their fortunes. I too cherished the idea of working in the Gulf.

A travel agent in the neighbourhood, also our client at the salon, helped me secure a visa and fixed up an interview with a company for a fee of ₹14,000 for a job. They wanted someone who was willing to slog. At the interview, I was asked about my experience in haircutting, shaving and my knowledge of English.

I nodded in the affirmative for everything except the last criterion. Imagine my joy when the interviewers said it did not matter since the new boss could not write or speak English. Feeling elated at getting the job, I made up my mind to learn the language my boss spoke, which was Arabic in the Doha-Qatar style.

I soon realised that things were not as easy as they had seemed to me. The core issue of generating finance for my travel needed to be resolved. My savings, amounted to only ₹7,000, while the payment for the agent's services was ₹14,000. I hoped Raghu would loan me the remaining amount. Most of my savings had been used up in renovating my village home to construct a fence, to lay floor tiles and get electricity connections, besides investing in gold for my mother.

Raghu refused to help. He feigned having no extra money to offer me a loan.

'From where do I get this amount? Do I keep so much money with me!' he retorted. I was aware that it was the miser in him talking; he was financially sound enough to lend me money if he wished, given his thriving business.

With no option, I pawned a gold chain and two finger rings with a jeweller across the road (also our client), briefing him on the work offer in Qatar. I assured him of repayment on my return and in case I failed to do so, I requested him to keep the gold as payment towards the loan. That night I spoke to Raghu, who had been giving me the cold shoulder all the while, about my new job in the Middle East.

'It is good to help people in trouble,' I said to Raghu, who chose to keep mum. 'I know that you have money stacked away in the cupboard. But it does not matter.'

I explained to Raghu the need to work in the Middle East where opportunities were many. I needed to earn well and save for my future. I also added that if I had been working so hard all this while, it was for my own sake and not for the benefit of others. Hence, I had to seek out better-paying jobs.

'I hope to do well (in Qatar). If I do well over there, then I plan to come back and set up my own business. In case I do not succeed, I will come back, perhaps come back to you,' I assured him. 'But at present, considering my circumstances, I would like to take leave of you.'

I am someone who is extremely devoted to my profession. I told Raghu that he too was good at his work, but I did not see in him the zeal and passion that I possessed for my work.

Raghu listened to me quietly. The next day he spoke to me again, gently reprimanding me about speaking out of turn with him. He said all that talk had been totally unnecessary.

'You know why I did not give you the money? You are like my right hand. What happens when one loses one's right hand? How does one feel?' he questioned, trying to convince me that he was a kind-hearted soul.

All said and done, Raghu was kind enough to see me off at the airport as I left for Qatar in 1984. He bid me goodbye with a smile on his face. As a farewell gesture, Vithal gifted me a watch with a cream-coloured dial and a golden strap. I was delighted because it was a unique piece.

Have the courage to follow your heart and intuition. They somehow already know what you truly want to become. Everything else is secondary.

—Steve Jobs, IT czar and co-founder of Apple Computers

chapter seven

GAINING A WEALTH OF EXPERIENCE IN THE GULF

My heart was fluttering with joy. I was bursting with happiness. I just could not stop smiling.

Ecstatic, I wanted to jump about after the job interview when I was told that I had landed an opportunity to work in Doha. It was my dream to work in the Gulf, and that dream was coming true. Tucking a couple of shirts and trousers into my trustworthy old red suitcase, I prepared to take the flight to Qatar from the international airport at Sahar in Mumbai.

While working in Mumbai, in my letters to my mother, I had discussed my plans to work in the Middle East. She too was of the opinion that a job overseas would better our prospects. For people in Mangalore and its surrounding towns and villages, working in the Gulf predictably meant discovering the proverbial pot of gold. There were many examples among our poor neighbours and other simple village folk of those who had worked in the Gulf for a few years and returned prosperous, effectively wiping out poverty from their lives. When she read that I had got a job in Doha, Mother was naturally pleased. I could sense her elation when I spoke to her later. She would talk to me from a call booth connected to our neighbour's phone in our hometown.

Qatar proved to be a turning point in my career.

That period of nearly four years, from October 1984 to August 1988, helped me become economically secure. Most importantly, I gained an enormous wealth of experience by honing my skills as a barber. Since making a phone call was expensive, I continued my written correspondence with my mother, describing my new life in a country where sand was in abundance and the atmosphere stiflingly hot.

At the end of the month, I would deposit my earnings in the village's Canara Bank Non-Resident Indian (NRI) account that my mother operated.

In Doha, initially, living conditions were oppressive. We were nine workers staying in a cramped dormitory, sleeping on bunk-beds and cooking food in the same room. In the backyard was a bath and a toilet, which had a makeshift door—a small plank covering only the top part of the entrance. When a person sat on the toilet seat, everyone could see him doing the job! It was awkward for us. However, we got used to the near-open system. We had no choice.

The company that had hired me to work at the sports club temporarily shifted my job to a building site. The club was under construction and not entirely functional. I was quite comfortable with the arrangement, although I found the job a backbreaking task. Wearing rubber gumboots and hand gloves, I assisted in painting, clearing cement debris, and loading and unloading cement bricks at the building site.

I laboured as a 'helper' for nearly eight months. The bricks that I had to carry were heavy, yet I hauled them with all my strength to complete the work. Being the youngest worker, my seniors, who saw me toil, advised that I approach our superiors to seek a transfer to a department that was less cumbersome.

I was hesitant to voice my problem because I feared it might sound like a grievance. I was earning a tidy amount of

₹3,000 on conversion to Indian currency. What if my superiors misunderstood and decided to deport me back to India? That would shatter my dreams of working in the Gulf region. My mother would be devastated. And what would people in my village say about my deportation? They would poke fun at me, turning me into an object of ridicule. All kinds of bizarre thoughts scurried across my mind. I stayed put in the same position where I was working.

The following month, I bought a pair of scissors, a comb and a razor. The idea was to offer a barber's services of haircutting and shaving to roommates and workers at the construction site every week on a holiday. The idea worked to their advantage since a barber was literally coming to their doorstep. They were mostly poor labourers, so I only charged a small fee. I reckoned that, just like me, they would be saving to send money to their families back home.

I started my part-time work on the sandy shores of the Persian Gulf every Friday, the weekly holiday there, with a pair of scissors, a comb and a plastic stool for clients to sit on while I worked on their mane. Trimming hair, beards and shaving did eventually create a bit of a mess around the place. Just so that the owners of the site would not find an excuse to reprimand me, I would clean the area by collecting this strewn hair in a plastic bag on my way back to the room. Later, the rubbish was dumped in the dirt bin.

When the Al Sadd Sports Club opened, I commenced my job as an operator at the front office desk. With some knowledge of the Arabic language, I was able to attend to phone calls and transfer lines to members visiting the club. I understood a fair amount of English; I had picked it up in Mumbai while decoding English sentences into Kannada, with the help of *Rapidex*.

The swanky club, a hub of outdoor and indoor games, had

several international sportsmen playing volleyball, football, hockey, table tennis, lawn tennis and squash. Their coaches too visited the club, giving me an opportunity to watch the games and meet all of them personally.

After my working hours, I was allowed to play at the ground. Though I tried my hand at all the games, my favourite was football. As a young boy, deprived of recreational activities, my exposure to games had only gone as far as turning the pages of sports magazines read by clients in salons. But now, I could finally give in to the childlike yearning I had in me, to hold and kick the ball. The manager of the club, Atif Riz, a gracious person, was extremely pleased with my work. In the club's guestroom, a rather large place, he set up a temporary salon by fitting large mirrors and a comfortable chair. Riz would describe me as an 'engineer' of haircuts while recommending me to visitors. He even took me to his bungalow to cut and trim the hair of his family members.

What impressed him was that I was willing to undertake any odd job with enthusiasm and see it to its completion. Apart from handing me the duties of phone operator and barber, he also entrusted me with the responsibility of cleaning the entire club premises. I carried out all his orders without hesitation.

As the days passed, my clientele at the salon got bigger, merely by word of mouth. The wealthy people frequenting the club were charged ten rials for a haircut, but my charges for construction workers never changed. Every Friday, I went to the seashore with my tools, alternating between two locations—one where I worked earlier, and the other a building site where a friend, Achyuta Achari, worked. His co-workers queued up for shaves and haircuts. Achari, a skilled carpenter, is now a reputed name in the furniture business in Mangalore.

In a short while, I was cutting and styling the hair of coaches and players who dropped by at the club for practice sessions and games. The clientele for whom I cut, shaved, trimmed, sheared, clipped and styled began to look like a global mix. Besides local Qataris, there were people from many different nationalities, including European, Brazilian, Tunisian, Turkish, Iranian, Egyptian, Filipino, Korean, Pakistani, Bangladeshi, Sri Lankan and Indian.

Long, short, straight, thick, curly, rough, smooth, silky, spiky, wavy, spring, ring and sometimes a mix of these varieties—there was every hair type for me to cut and shape. I handled natural hair of varied hues—black, brown, grey and blonde. Managing the hair of people belonging to different countries and the experience of handling such a wide range of textures available in one place was rich and invaluable to me.

This international exposure that allowed me to work on so many hair types was tremendously useful. Most importantly, I understood that the quality of hair determined the type of haircut that might be most suitable for a client. The knowledge in hair diversity also helped me ascertain problems that trouble the hair or scalp. Today, I can advise clients about hair management and consequent remedies to keep a healthy mane. It fine-tuned my skills as a barber. Financially, the extra workload definitely added to my income, and experientially, it set me rolling on the path to becoming a proficient hairdresser.

Sportsmen visiting the club would fix appointments with me, preferring to have their hair done in their rooms, rather than the salon of the five-star hotel they were staying in. When they were happy with my work they would gift me T-shirts, watches, sunglasses and track pants. My wardrobe was beginning to look like a mini shop, full of clothes and accessories of varied international brands.

My work was progressing in full swing. It filled me with a sense of profound accomplishment. After struggling for years right from childhood, I had finally begun to enjoy the sweet fruits of labour now, in my late twenties. Working through the day and playing at the sports ground late in the evening, I truly enjoyed my stint. I made many friends, went to their homes, tasted local cuisine and relished the warm weather that appealed to my health. Even though it was sizzling hot in Doha, I felt comfortable. As I mentioned earlier, I utterly dislike cold climes.

An unforgettable experience would be the visit to the mansion of a sheikh of the renowned Khalifa family. I could not believe my eyes when I noticed the luxuriant lifestyle they led amidst opulent settings. The high ceiling, grand chandeliers, ornate lamps, rich cushions, expensive drapes and soft carpets left me spellbound. One step on the carpet and my foot would sink four inches below. Was this real, I wondered.

In school, my history books were filled with depictions of ostentation and the grandeur of palaces belonging to kings and queens. Suddenly it felt like all those pages were coming alive in front of me! I was dumbfounded for quite some time. I saw a display of massive ornamentally designed vessels filled with the local coffee called *ghawa*. Later, I visited this place several times, choosing to drink only Coke.

Doha offered an exceptional range of good-quality food, exotic vegetables, non-vegetarian dishes, dry fruits, cakes, ice creams and chocolates. I tasted the entire food palette available. However, I did miss having my mother around. I would have liked her to experience the gourmet spread and the rich diversity I was witnessing. To some extent, my mother did get to taste international food fare in Mumbai, where we set up our new home after my return to India from Qatar. I would take her out for a meal to introduce her to new dishes—Maharashtrian, North Indian, Italian, Thai, Chinese and Mexican. All these cuisines were very different from her South Indian cooking methods, except for Thai, which she thought came close to her delectable coconut curries.

I would summarise my stay in Qatar as one of the best phases in my life. The work experience, food, accommodation and above all the people for whom I worked for at the stadium salon, who were caring and gentle, made my Qatar stay memorable. Qatar in a way set a high benchmark for me in my future endeavours. I learnt that hair textures varied according to cultures, countries and continents and I also understood how to cut and manage different types of hair. Now I had to devise how to give those trendy and stylish cuts that I would so often see in international fashion magazines available at the salon. I knew that I still had to learn a lot more about the coiffeur's field of work.

Young Shiva with his mother, clicked in a photo studio

An old photo of Shiva's mother in their village

The house in which Shiva was born

St. Lawrence Primary Kannada School where
Shiva studied upto Class Five

Shiva's mother worked in the tailoring unit of this shop

The house in his native place, where a young Shiva and his mother worked as labourers when it was being built

Shiva undertook the death-defying feat of stepping down to clean the bottom of this deep well located in Kariminabai's garden

Acres and acres of lush tea gardens and areca plantations at Yelemadalu

The home of Shiva's uncle at Yelemadalu

The barber shop where Shiva worked as a young boy is now closed down

Shiva would hide the little money he earned in this hollow alcove above the salon wall

Ajanta Salon, Bhandup, where
Shiva worked when he first arrived in Mumbai

Shiva found solace at this stream opposite his uncle's house

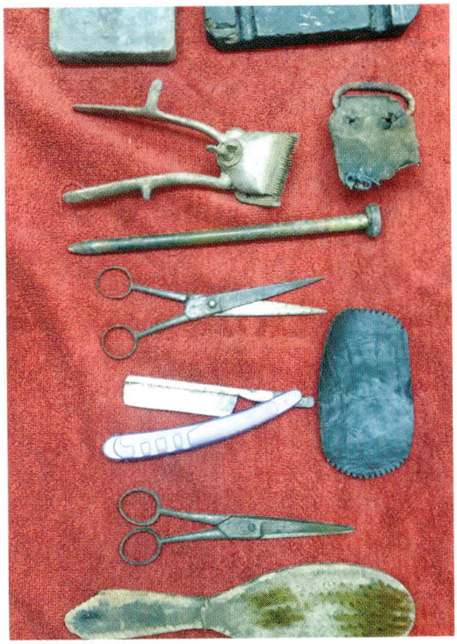

Tools that Shiva used as a young barber

Before leaving for Qatar, Shiva managed this barber's shop owned by Raghu Bhandary in Bhandup, Mumbai

Shiva's parlour in Matunga, Mumbai

Shiva with his first wife, late Harinakshi

Take up one idea. Make that one idea your life—think of it, dream of it, live on that idea. Let the brain, muscles, nerves, every part of your body, be full of that idea, and just leave every other idea alone. This is the way to success.

—*Swami Vivekananda, social reformer and philosopher*

chapter eight

LEARNING THE PROFESSIONAL WAY

Humorous, awkward and bizarre—that is how I would sum up my interaction with the visa officials at the Mumbai office of the British Deputy High Commission. They would ask me a question and I would reply with my rehearsed answers. I could not understand what they said and they could not figure out my replies. There was utter confusion. I realised I was in a soup! I did not comprehend a word in English!

I promptly showed them the letter of admission to a course I wanted to enrol in, in the UK, and newspaper clippings featuring my latest award. I had won the first prize at the Wild and Wacky Hairshow Contest organised by Salon International at the World Peace Award 1998 competition held at the World Trade Centre in Mumbai.

One of the judges, Christopher Mann, Chairman – Fellowship of British Hairdressing, and Commissioner – Salon International, was really impressed with my work. I had created a peace symbol on the back of a model's head and shaded it with colours. It was Christopher who had advised me to apply for an advanced course at the Vidal Sassoon Academy in London. And there I was, hoping with all my might that the visa be granted to me smoothly.

I then showed the officials photographs of my other creative work that included ingenious designs carved out on clients' hair. For instance, I had snipped one customer's hair using a 'buzz effect' to create a soccer field with players while on another customer's mane, I had made a basketball court. At the back of yet another client's head, I had created the notorious bandit Veerappan's handlebar moustache. I also showed them the photograph of the award-winning peace symbol.

After seeing the pictures, they gave me a pleased look. The visa officials understood the reason for my travel. Sifting through my papers, the officials started smiling and talking among themselves animatedly. Language was a barrier as I could not make sense of what they were saying; however, I understood that they approved of my work. One official asked me, with the help of gestures, if I could do a similar cut for him. I nodded enthusiastically. They appeared totally satisfied and granted me the visa!

The World Peace Award was not merely an accolade for my creative work but a blessing in disguise. It paved the way for a hugely creative and rewarding career, and moulded me into a leading coiffeur, stylist, specialist, designer and an artist in the arena of hair and beauty care. It opened up numerous avenues of work. In my career, I have received several awards in recognition of my work, but the prestigious peace award was the first in my life, and hence, the most special.

At the international hairstyle competition, one of my clients, a college boy named Thomas, became my model. Earlier, I had styled his hair for a photo shoot he was working on to prepare a modelling portfolio. It was on the back of his head that I had designed the peace symbol and filled it with colours. It looked like a shining star. It was the first time I used colours on someone's head. I filled colourful beads in the front portion of his hair giving him a slight Afro look. The Om symbol printed on Thomas's shirt completed the look of a very free-spirited person. I worked with a female model named Supriya, whose hair was knotted with flowers woven in them. The complete appearance articulated the concept of freedom, truly reminiscent of the flower power days of the '60s.

We received a standing ovation from all the judges as Thomas walked the ramp to illustrate the peace theme. Ruby Bhatia, who was a video jockey with a leading music channel and one of the judges, clapped for the longest time. Now I was certain that the judges had liked my work. But I kept praying that I win the round, for it looked like the other participants were giving me tough competition with their bold and outlandish designs.

One contestant sported colourful long stripes that looked like the dreadlocks of a rock star, another wore painted scarves tied stylishly on the head, like Rastafarians do, and one candidate even emulated Karnataka's traditional dance form, Yakshagana, complete with a colourful face mask. The stage sparkled with vibrant hues and patterns.

Before stepping on the stage, as he saw other contestants dazzle, Thomas became nervous and began doubting his own chances of winning the round. I convinced him to regain his confidence and put his best foot forward. Sure enough, by the evening, when the judges announced that we had won the first prize, we were in a celebratory mood. The judges further lauded the fact that we had used only hair to make the design and not contraptions to enhance the appearance.

Christopher Mann encouraged me to attend a training course in the UK and shared his email address to contact him for more information. I took his word seriously and corresponded with him via emails to further understand the procedure to secure admission at the Vidal Sassoon Academy in London.

The same year, I attended a weeklong course at the premier academy located at Marble Arch in London. It was the first time I was attending a class after leaving school as a child. I was excited and at the same time nervous about learning new hairstyles and trends in vogue on the international fashion scene. I was sure the course would be an out-of-the-world experience.

And most certainly, it turned out to be one. The ultimate destination of creativity had opened its doors for me; I could walk in and give my ideas new expression with absolute abandon. As I walked into class on my first day there, my heart was beating fast. Through the day, I was exposed to a mindboggling number of hairdos. Gobsmacked, I could not believe my eyes. I watched, fascinated by a wide collection of the most creative styles I had ever seen, sported by live models posing on the ramp.

The academy gave me access to the latest fashion brochures and magazines. It was not as if I had not been exposed to foreign magazines showcasing hairstyles; I had handled a plethora of hair types belonging to people of diverse nationalities at the salon in Doha's sports club. Working at the swish place had already given me ample exposure to upmarket international style glossies.

But at the academy, I was witness to those hairstyles being created in front of me. Teachers were continuously demonstrating different hairstyling techniques. Models were specifically called in during the course so that we could give expression to our vision by trying out some extraordinary hairdos on them. I could let my imagination soar to astounding heights. I experimented with a range of cuts, tried out colours and used almost all hairstyling products.

In my mind, I was comparing some of the chic international styles with the ones prevalent in India. In the '80s, people were not as adventurous as they are now. Women liked a bit of styling and men preferred the staid look. Whereas abroad, people with short hair were more than willing to experiment with new ideas. Imagine my wonderment when I saw a bob cut take a different meaning when one part was coloured in a new tinge and the other remained in the original colour. Or when a bulk of hair was left loose hanging at the sides, like the ears of a sheep, giving the short hair a novel feel.

Would anyone in India be bold and try out such hairstyles? Come to think of it, even in the late '90s, clients were conservative about sporting radical styles. Most women had long hair and preferred only a snip here or a cut there to give it a little bounce and shape. When I saw the fringe on the forehead, it reminded me of parents in India wanting their children to have the 'Rasna cut', after the child artiste modelled with a fringe in the soft drink advertisement in the early '90s. And before that, the fringe was 'Sadhana cut', a household name after the late Bollywood actress who donned the style in most of her films, aping Hollywood's luminary, the late Audrey Hepburn. It's only now that I see customers asking for quirky and unconventional cuts.

In the weeklong course, I learnt many techniques and the finer nuances of styling. I learnt to use high-powered blow-dryers, various combs, scissors, brushes, highlights and the art of colouring. I learnt to differentiate between a pedal brush and a tele-comb, colouring and global highlighting, and the appropriate uses of serum, mousse and spray. In structuring, I learnt the professional way of holding hair at angles of 90 degrees at the back and 60 degrees at the side while giving cuts.

I noticed that most westerners had thin and soft hair over a rather sensitive scalp. The skin on the head had a tender feel because of overexposure to various products and their constituent chemicals. It was imperative to know how to use the comb gently over the scalp, taking great care to neither pull nor tug at the hair while loosening knots. Such rough practices of forceful combing are commonplace in India. In villages, women draw the comb hard and strong on the scalp and tie the hair up into a tight knot or braid. Our scalps are strong enough to bear harsh combing.

Europeans, I realised, like to stress on the importance of presentation of style. Even with minimal hair, they groomed themselves exceedingly well and always appeared smart and fashionable.

I was taught to shampoo and condition hair by giving a backwash without putting the client through any inconvenience. I was careful not to drop water or chemical products on the person's face or body.

The uniform at the academy—a black overcoat—instilled a sense of pride and looked very respectful. To my mind, the attire gave dignity and recognition to our profession, just as the black and white coats that lawyers and doctors wear, setting them apart as distinguished professionals.

During the training programme, I also observed people's flair for clothing and changing hairstyles. Even the receptionist at the lobby wore a fancy hairdo each day. It did not matter that there were only a few strands on the head; the hair had to be well cut, coloured and fashionable. That awareness is now spreading in India.

My biggest drawback was my English. I was not as familiar with the language back then as I am today. A lot of the study matter was written on blackboards in the classroom. How could I understand and decipher the language? I did not want to miss out on any information. It worried me a little in the beginning, but I could not let that become an obstacle in my learning process.

Teachers were aware of my challenges and were helpful and cooperative in explaining lessons to me. I was never reluctant to approach instructors. I needed to learn about all the wide-ranging styles and new products, so I would repeatedly ask questions to get the clarity I needed. They would answer and explain willingly by speaking deliberately in a slow manner so that I could grasp every word.

In a class of twelve students, some from Belgium and Greece, I was the only Indian and the only one who did not know the language as well as the others. To overcome the problem, I would listen to lectures using headphones provided in the class in order to concentrate better. As the teachers explained theory lessons, using the headphones helped me comprehend each spoken word. Back home I would listen to the same recording repeatedly until I clearly understood what was said in the programme. Practical sessions were the easiest for me as I could learn simply by watching demonstrations. I would apply those techniques and styling products to create designs on the hair of models who were there as part of the curriculum. My teachers were very happy with my work.

When a model was satisfied with the hairstyle I created for her, she would thank me and give me a peck on my cheek to express her happiness. This gesture was new to me. I would simply smile back at their show of appreciation.

On the last day of our course we were awarded with a certificate and after that, the occasion was celebrated by popping champagne. I had worn a suit for the occasion. Everyone complimented me on my attire and said I looked handsome. It made me feel nice. Our main instructor saw a small hair strand jutting out over my ear. He thought it was rather unusual, although I did not pay attention to it. He quickly took a cordless trimmer and snipped the odd bit.

'Now it looks perfect,' he commented. With a broad smile, I said, 'Thank you.' In the academy, I noticed that people often thanked each other to reciprocate a kind gesture. I was keen to learn their manners and hence made a conscious effort to emulate such simple etiquettes and use them in my daily interactions.

I stayed in London for nearly a month with my hosts Purshottam Sota, his wife Kumudben, their sons Rahul and Ashik, and daughter Priya with her husband Bhavesh Kotak, an orthopaedic doctor.

I toured London after the course, taking in the sights and scenes of the foreign country and imbibing the fashion sense of the locals. While walking on the road, my eyes would first spot the mane. What have they done with their tresses? A combination of updo hairstyles was most popular, perhaps because working women found it practical and easy while commuting to their workplaces.

There were a variety of updos to be seen—some tied their hair into a bun, a knot, a chignon or even a ponytail. The updo is one style that provides comfort to the wearer and ensures minimum chance of the hair getting messy. An updo looks neat, tidy and lends a soft elegance to women. Hence, it is also a preferred style for a formal event like a wedding party. Sometimes enhanced with pearls, curls, tiny plaits or any sort of bling accessory, it adds to the party look.

Another trend that seemed very popular was piercing—ear-piercing was common, just as it is with Indians, but seeing the lips, eyes, eyebrows and the navel pierced were a first for me and I thought they were crazy to maim their body parts like that. Tattoos were another rage, colourfully drawn all over the body. The use of henna paste to make temporary tattoo designs was a revelation. One could make designs on the feet, hands, legs, neck and forehead using henna. I quite liked the idea.

Though I was fascinated with the country for its elegance, sense of fashion, standard of living and keenness shown by working professionals to grow in their respective fields, it was also a culture shock for someone like me who came from a traditional Indian setup. Young girls and boys smoking like they had no care in the world disturbed and shocked me immensely.

I was amazed to know that children left their parents' homes at the age of eighteen to live independently. In India, it is the opposite. At eighteen we are still attached to our parents and even later we prefer to stay with them and look after them. In fact, when I leave home each day, I imperatively touch my mother's feet, seek her blessings, and only then do I set out. In the West, family attachments differ; they prefer to behave like friends.

On my way back to India, I took a two-day stopover in Dubai to tour and shop around the place. I picked up several gadgets that I thought would be useful for my work, such as a face massager, acne remover, some cosmetic products and a mobile phone. I generously spent money, buying scissors, brushes and other accessories in London too as I am fond of investing in appliances related to my field of work. I still use those scissors for my clients.

A certificate from a reputed academy was without doubt an achievement; it made me feel extremely elated and the knowledge that I gained in the process was invaluable. Back in Mumbai though, the question that bothered me was—how much of what I had learnt could I use on my clients? Although the technical aspects of my learning were timeless and would always remain useful, a major part of my study had involved learning about high fashion. I was a little unsure of how receptive my Indian clients would be to my newly acquired skills.

In India, women usually preferred either blow-drying or curling their hair. I took this opportunity to use hairdryers and curlers to the maximum, by making a little change here and there with hair strands. I tried layering long hair; this was yet to become a rage. I would give an in-turn in the front and an out-turn at the back. For short hair, I tried keeping a few strands in the front long and keeping the hair at the back very short. Above all, to date, I sincerely follow tips taught by my alma mater, the Vidal Sassoon Academy, regarding hair care, cuts, styles and fashion.

The three ordinary things that we often don't pay enough attention to, but which I believe are the drivers of all success, are hard work, perseverance and basic honesty.

—Azim Premji, Chairman – Wipro Limited, and czar of the Indian IT industry

chapter nine

WELL-WISHERS—SHARING AN EMOTIONAL BOND

Late Balasaheb Thackeray, Founder and Supremo of the Political Party, Shiv Sena

Many years ago, at a film awards event, I saw Saheb—that is how everyone addressed the late Balasaheb Thackeray—sitting in the front row with a group of alert bodyguards standing behind. I noticed that he had an impressive personality and a smiling demeanour, yet there was something very intimidating about his presence. I had always been fascinated by the prospect of being established enough to groom well-known personalities. To date, whenever I notice a renowned figure, my mind begins to conjure up creative hairstyles that would suit the individual's persona. Similarly, when I saw Saheb, I began wondering how I would have styled his hair and beard.

Lo and behold! Many years later, one fine day, I got a call to attend to Saheb because his usual hairstylist was on leave.

I could not believe my ears. *I* was called to do *Saheb*'s beard! During our first meeting, he asked me a barrage of questions—What is your name? Where do you hail from? How many years have you been working in Mumbai? Do you like

Marathi? Do you understand or speak the language? Finally, he decided he would speak only in Marathi with me. I had learnt the language while working in a salon in Bhandup, but the Marathi spoken in the neighbourhood used to be laced with profanities. I was not particularly good at conversing, but I could manage.

As my visits became frequent, my Marathi got better after speaking with Saheb; from him I learnt the finer nuances and purity of the language. He was a very talkative person. When he spoke, I would merely listen to him, nodding my head while taking in every word he uttered. In return, he expected an answer only in Marathi.

The first time I finished working on his beard and hair, he looked into the mirror for a very long time. He was very conscious of his appearance and liked to have every strand in place. Then he turned around and gave me an appraising look. He said, '*Chhaaan* (lovely),' dragging out the aaa in unmistakable satisfaction.

He said that I was confident wielding scissors in my hands and asked me to come whenever he called for me. I felt extremely happy that he had appreciated my work.

I used to give an oval shape to his beard, which I thought matched his personality. As for his hair, it required a slight trim occasionally.

Once, when I was out of Mumbai, his secretary called me, saying that Saheb wanted me to do his beard. I expressed my inability to make it that day, promising to be there the very day I got back to the city. On my return, he called me to say that he was not happy with the work done by another hairdresser.

'*Wat laun takli* (ruined it),' he exclaimed in Marathi, unhappy with the person who had done his beard and hair in my absence. The person's hands were shivering and he boasted that he was an award-winning hairdresser—Saheb complained about the man.

He told me that from then on, whenever I planned to travel out of Mumbai, I should keep his secretary informed so that in case my services were required, I could be called before I left the city. And so, each time I intended to travel out of Mumbai, I would make a call to Matoshri (Saheb's residence) to find out if I was needed. This practice continued for as long as he lived. I admire the fact that in all those years, he did not cancel an appointment even once.

He liked to chat about a range of topics, and that included making enquiries about my family, work and health. He would ask with curiosity whether I had dosa and coconut chutney, our staple breakfast. That morning, perhaps he could smell my fingers still bearing a whiff of lentils and coconut, while I was doing his beard. He made small and intriguing observations about people and things around him.

I had purchased a flat in Oshiwara and had mentioned to him that it was only a four-bedroom apartment. 'You forgot to mention the kitchen!' he had chuckled, with a glint in his eyes. I could not stop smiling. He always had to have the last say.

His talks would be interlaced with my name. He would begin the sentence with 'Shiva…', intersperse our conversation with 'Shiva…' off and on, and end it too with 'Shiva…'. That was his way of speaking and I liked it tremendously. It gave me a sense of belonging.

I felt grateful that I had come to Mumbai to make a living from a village far away, and here I was, grooming a very important person. I consider myself fortunate. The times that I have spent with him are among my most memorable experiences.

Each time I touched his feet during my visit, he would shower me with blessings, letting his hands rest on my head for a long time. I felt that his blessings had a powerful impact on my life since he had only good words to say.

Somewhere in the middle of a conversation during a haircut, he would randomly throw a question at me and wait for my answer. To my ordinary reply, he would simply remark, 'Chhaan!' His reaction would leave me bewildered. Had I really given an appropriate reply, I would wonder.

I understood that he had a very sharp memory because he could recollect and narrate several events and situations while speaking to me. As a token of respect, I would carry jasmine flowers, which he admired. Saheb would promptly place them in front of the photographs of the family deity and of Meenatai, his late wife.

Often, he would run his fingers through his tuft in the front to keep it neatly in place. That was his hallmark style.

An interview based on my work as a hairstylist was published in Shiv Sena's party newspaper *Saamna*. The morning that it appeared in the paper, he called me up at around 9.15 to ask: 'Have you seen your interview in *Saamna*?' I felt truly humbled by the fact that such a big personality should call me up personally to tell me about the piece published on me.

He directed his son Uddhav and grandchildren Aditya and Tejas to get their hair done by me.

After he passed away, I felt like I had lost a close member of my family. I do miss him a lot. Even today, when I visit Matoshri, I can distinctly feel his lingering presence in the house.

Uddhav Thackeray, Chief of Shiv Sena

Uddhavji is a soft-spoken person who likes to wear a casual haircut. He is a kind-hearted soul and a man of few words. When I try to make suggestions to him about his look, he smiles in response and tells me that he is happy to keep it simple. I like to colour his grey hair although he says he prefers the natural look. He has tremendous respect and love for his father.

Uddhavji's wife, Rashmiji, on the other hand, is a dynamic person who likes to talk about her children and family. She always enquires about my mother's health and my work at the salons. When we meet, we discuss a great deal about natural foods and their health benefits—like the importance of fresh curd in daily meals. An extremely good host, she likes to ensure that all her guests are treated well.

To Aditya, the elder son, I try to give a corporate cut with a slightly messy look, while the younger son, Tejas, is more fashionable. He is the tallest in the family and a football enthusiast with a penchant for using natural products. He likes to keep up with the latest trends. I give him different styles each time I do his hair.

Madhur Bhandarkar, National Award-Winning Filmmaker & Padma Shri Awardee

When Madhur Bhandarkar came to my salon at Lokhandwala, his first movie *Chandni Bar* was making headlines for its realistic portrayal of Mumbai's dance bars. He had walked in for a shave. Later, he began stopping by more often, saying he was satisfied with services offered at Shiva's salon, and we struck a friendly rapport. When he won the first national award for his film, he called me to share the news, saying that he was extremely elated.

He has an endearing personality which makes one feel very comfortable talking to him. Over the years, I have experimented a lot with his hair, which has a rough texture, by giving varied subtle cuts to his thick mop. Once, when he was to attend an award function, I snipped the sides short. He appreciated the style. However, he prefers the corporate-style sleek appearance of hair neatly smoothed down in place with gel. It is a comfortable look that puts him at ease. As a director, perforce he may have a big event to attend or a social visit to make, all in one day. Being a celebrity, he is watched by people all the time. When he visits my salon, other customers enquire about him and some approach him for autographs.

Madhur Sir—my first connection with Bollywood—has been instrumental in introducing me to several well-known personalities in the film industry. I always look forward to the launch of his new films. I was present during the making of *Fashion* and *Dil Toh Baccha Hai Ji.* He likes to introduce me as: '*Yeh mera struggling period ka dost hai* (he is my friend from my earlier days of struggle).'

In the film *Heroine*, he has included a clip shot of me at Shiva's Academy, as the hairstylist of the leading actress Kareena Kapoor. For *Calendar Girls*, he has shown me as the hairstylist in the film's title track, and in *Indu Sarkar*, I play the role of a prominent businessman in a party scene. Madhur Sir likes to include me in his films, perhaps as a token of our friendship.

I find him to be a down-to-earth person, a family man, a doting father to his daughter and a loving husband to his wife Renu.

Mahesh Shetty, Chairman and MD, MT Educare

In 1993, Mahesh Anna visited my Mulund parlour for a haircut and ever since, he has been frequenting Shiva's salons. His pupils, who visited my salon, told me that Mahesh Anna talked about me in his tutorial classes held at Mulund and Chembur. The example was part of a small lesson about how I aimed to become an entrepreneur. The suffix 'anna' (elder brother in Kannada and Tulu, as also other South Indian languages) is usually used as a mark of respect.

'Shiva is now a well-known hairstylist. He sowed a seed in the form of a tiny shop, and that has blossomed into a series of salons,' is how he speaks of me to bolster students' ambitions. 'With a little initiative, you too can make it big,' he would tell them.

I always look forward to his visits to my salon. When I have an idea, I am keen to share and discuss it with him and seek his advice on the matter. We have long conversations regarding my future business plans, and he often encourages me to move with the times. He quotes some of the world's top businessmen, narrating their personal stories as examples of achieving success. Each time I meet him, I feel like I have learnt something new.

He speaks in a low and measured tone. He has an aura that commands tremendous respect among people. A thorough gentleman who speaks fluent English, and chaste Kannada and Tulu, he communicates succinctly. I listen to him intently and absorb every word he says.

He makes it a point to chat with my staff, enquires after them and advises them to value money. He tells them to inculcate the habit of saving a large portion of their salary and to introduce discipline in their lives to abstain from spending needlessly despite many temptations.

Mahesh Anna's son Prithvi and wife Rupa have been a tremendous source of encouragement to me.

Ashok Dhamankar, Director, Magna Publications

A soft-spoken, well-mannered and nattily dressed person, Dhamankar Sir is someone who will go out of his way to help people. He has been in the publication business for a long time and his association with the glamorous world of films also stretches far, which is why when I need any advice in these areas of work, I go to him and he is ever-willing to hear me out. We became friends during his visits to my salons.

He is a man of few words, but when he speaks, it literally touches my heart. He advises me on conduct and professional etiquette, gives ideas to promote my brand Shiva's, invites my team of stylists to assist in the annual awards function of the film glossy *Stardust* and other publications, and never fails to be there for me, unfailingly lending his support at the opening of my salons. He is extremely intuitive about hardworking people and appreciates the diligence and approach I bring to my profession.

William Sequeira, Vice-Chairman, Model Cooperative Bank Ltd.

William Sir came to my salon in Mulund for a haircut in 1993. We got chatting in Tulu, since both of us hail from towns adjoining Mangalore. While taking leave, he said that he stayed in the same high-rise, so if ever I wanted any help, I could approach him without hesitation.

Ever since, he has been advising me on financial matters and guiding me to procure bank loans for my businesses. He is a dear friend and guide and I feel very fortunate to have someone like him to look out for me.

He has the exceptional quality of being a patient listener and promptly comes up with solutions to any problem. He is a mild-mannered person and, at the same time, always jovial. He can make one smile even when one is badly bogged down by a difficult situation. He can discern genuine entrepreneurs and makes a huge effort to assist them financially by facilitating loans from the bank.

My business plans to start a branch at Lokhandwala, the third in the series of Shiva's salons, appealed to him immensely after I discussed details of the venture that would offer innovative new services, especially to the glamorous world of television and film personalities in the vicinity. He helped me secure a large loan for the purpose.

His wife Janet, son Kenith and daughter Karen are like an extended family to me, and they never miss wishing me during Diwali. I call to wish them on Christmas. When Harinakshi was unwell, she used to enjoy talking to them because they would always try to buoy up her spirits in those dark days.

Vinod Chopra, Businessman

My friendship with Vinodji too started at the salon when he visited for a haircut. He likes to maintain a corporate look with the shirt always tucked in and formal trousers. In keeping with his personality, I give him a sleek look. Since we are both businessmen, we have always been able to relate well to each other. He advises me on how to develop my brand in different ways. He tells me to be open to the idea of granting franchises to entrepreneurs interested in setting up Shiva's outlets.

He also advises me on legal issues owing to his law background. He has stood by me through my difficult times. During Harinakshi's illness, he would accompany us on our hospital visits. He came along with me to Benares to immerse Harinakshi's ashes after her passing away. He did not want to leave me alone. He has been a great source of strength at all times in my life.

Do what you do so well that they will want to see it again and bring their friends.

—Walt Disney, Disney Productions

chapter ten

MAGIC IN SHIVA'S FINGERS—PATRONS SPEAK

Satish Shah, Businessman, Kampala, Uganda

Shiva has magic in his fingers. People say Goddess Saraswati resides in Lata Mangeshkar's throat; I say Goddess Saraswati resides in Shiva's hands. He is committed to his work with all his soul. I have tried many hairdressers—you worry about what they may do the moment they touch you. But Shiva is an exception. His fingers are soft as a feather. The moment he starts cutting your hair, you don't feel anything other than complete relaxation.

Whenever I visit India, he cuts my hair. I have been his customer for the last seven years. I travel to India at least five times a year, and since I stay near the Juhu salon, I make it a point to get my hair done from Shiva's. I do not visit any other salon.

Shiva colours my hair like he is painting a portrait. His hands are confident, they do not shake. And his work is so precise and clean that my clothes never bear stains from the chemical in the colour. I spotted his salon quite by chance while I was travelling to town on Juhu Tara road, and dropped by impulsively to get my hair done.

On my first visit to the Juhu salon, the staff told me that Mr Shiva was their boss, but he was not there. I thought to myself that I wanted him, and only him, to cut my hair and so I insisted. Shiva made time for me later. Ever since, I always taken an appointment before visiting the salon, and he has never failed to make himself available. This is his dedication.

✂

Roshini Kotari, Media Marketing Professional, Mumbai

The first time I got my hair cut by Shiva, I remember that it was a complete makeover for me. My look changed totally. I had waist-length hair which he chopped considerably, making it look grungy and a bit wild. I just loved it. I had never seen myself this way.

That was more than fifteen years ago, when I was studying in junior college. I continue to visit his salons at Mulund, Lokhandwala and Juhu, and I trust only Shiva with my hair. When I go for a haircut, I don't tell him what I am looking for and neither does he try to make an impression by showing pictures of numerous styles. He decides what suits my personality and how best it will compliment the wavy texture of my hair. My problems of split-ends and persistent dandruff too stopped after following Shiva's advice on how to care for the scalp.

I use a lot of colour, such as shades of red and gold, pink and purple, or any other combination on my hair. Shiva likes to experiment with colours within the limits of what looks best. I completely trust his ability. At one point, he had shortened my hair to neck-length, but now I keep a shoulder-length style. My entire family—father, husband, brother and US-based sister—get their haircuts from Shiva.

I am someone who is always on the go, with little time

to spend doing up my hair. I hardly ever comb my hair, preferring to run my fingers through, un-knotting strands. Shiva understands my reluctance to spare time for hair maintenance. He gives me cuts that are easy to maintain and look smart.

✂

Riya Pariani, Homemaker, Mumbai

I had frizzy hair which I would straighten in parlours for a soft look. For many years, I retained the straight look, until I visited Shiva's at Juhu in the year 2000, where my perception about maintaining hair totally changed. Shiva advised me, judging the quality of my hair, to keep it natural and resist using heavy-duty electrical gadgets that cause more harm. I like the fact that to date, he gives me honest opinions.

Now my hair is not as crimped but still wavy with curls at the ends. Shiva styles my hair in uneven steps, making the best of the up-and-down nature of my mane. I trust his decision totally because I feel he has magic in his fingers. He decides how to cut and the result is wonderful.

✂

Amit Mehta, Businessman/Restaurateur, Pune

In the year 1992, I was introduced to Shiva by a common friend at his Mulund parlour. Ever since that day, I have never got haircuts from anybody else. In 2005, I shifted to Pune with my family. I travel to Mumbai specially to get a haircut from Shiva, once in every six or seven weeks, when I feel that my hair is growing out and needs a trim. I fix an appointment with him, calling from Pune prior to my visit, and drop in at any of the parlours at Mulund, Lokhandwala or Juhu, whichever is convenient for Shiva.

Once I sit on the chair in his salon, I feel completely relaxed. Shiva decides what looks best on me. In keeping with the trend, he gives a medium-short haircut, but keeps it shorter at the back. Over the years, I feel a strong bond has been established between both of us. I feel for him like I would for a brother. My father and sister also visit his salons.

✂

Jitendra Veerchand Jain, Medical Shop Owner, Bhandup

I have known Shiva since the time he was working in a small salon called Ajanta in Bhandup. Our association goes back more than thirty years and that relationship still continues. He calls me Jeetubhai like everyone else and has cut my hair at Ajanta, when I used to frequent the place as a young man. When he opened his first salon in Thane, I became a regular and continued to patronise Shiva's after the Mulund branch opened, since it was very close to my house.

I have seen Shiva work very hard in the most difficult and poor conditions. We share some fond memories of the times when he worked in Bhandup. In those days, Shiva would drop by when he needed to print photocopies of some personal papers since I had a Xerox machine installed in my shop. Later at night, after work, we would meet behind my shop at a doodhwala's (milkman's) shop to drink milk with loads of cream. Over a glass of milk, we would chat and catch up on the day's work. I have visited his salons at Malad and Lokhandwala as well.

God could not be everywhere and therefore he made mothers.

—Rudyard Kipling, English writer and poet

chapter eleven

MOTHER—THE EPITOME OF SIMPLICITY

Uppigintha bere ruche illa, thayigintha devarilla

This Kannada saying displayed on a temple wall translates to: 'Nothing is tastier than salt and godlier than mother.'

What drew me towards temples was the free food served to devotees. Not being particularly religious, I visited only to have tasty meals that would fill my belly. After lunch, I would loiter around like a tourist, taking in the sights and reading quotations painted in calligraphic style on the walls. These shrines are ancient pieces of architecture, depicting idols, sculptures and figurines on pillars. Pictures and photographs of Hindu gods and goddesses are hung decoratively in a line across the walls.

The matter written on the walls conveyed deep meaning, mostly philosophical, which could be understood only after a thorough reading. I jotted the lines down in a book to memorise them. Time and again, I would ponder over those thought-provoking sayings. The above line about mothers is one such proverb that evoked tremendous emotion in me. After losing my father and sister in quick succession, my mother became my sole confidante and companion. And I became her strength and only support.

All her life, my mother persistently endured ordeals and

suffering. She experienced the pain of losing her parents at a very young age. During her short-lived wedded life, she stayed in the village most of the time, while my father worked in Mumbai. When she eventually joined him in the city, he was ailing, and after he passed away, she was burdened with two kids to look after. Weighed down by poverty, she could not afford to treat her daughter, who died of illness. Thereafter, she had to make innumerable sacrifices to look after me. She took up any job that came along—as a manual labourer at construction sites, stitching clothes, cooking in family kitchens and toiling in fields—all in the face of troubles, obstacles, jibes and deceit.

But the two of us have been together through thick and thin. I have been her only solace. I still get goose pimples as I mull over and talk about her tireless struggle. She is like a glowing lamp, radiating strength and instilling courage in the household. It is only because of her presence in my life that I have been able to reach thus far. I owe all the success in my professional career to my mother.

I have always made every effort possible to give her all the comforts of life. Now, at nearly eighty years of age, her days are more relaxed and she is at peace.

Writing this book has allowed us to strengthen our bond. We have been reliving our past by recollecting incidents, clarifying details of certain events, talking about our helplessness during our tragic circumstances when I was a child, recounting changes that took place later, analysing the drastic differences between our life in the village and in the city, and simply talking about our associations with distant relatives and their families. These topics usually come up for discussion at the dining table during meals which mainly consist of native Mangalorean food.

We have always been close to each other. But now we are able to discuss our past with an emotional ease that may have been difficult earlier when all our time was spent resolving problems.

Going down memory lane has its own pitfalls. Remembering any depressing incident from the past is like opening the floodgates of bad memories. There are too many in her life—from the time she got married at the early age of eighteen, stayed alone at her in-laws' place at Nitte while my father worked in Mumbai, to the shocking turn of events after Father's death, followed by hardships, deprivation and loneliness.

When she reminisces the past, she takes off on a tangent. At that point, it is rather difficult to control her thoughts and emotions. I guess her scars are too deep to fathom. I do manage to calm her down. She listens to my advice, holding every word close to her heart. Then, as if to put an end to the thoughts of our bleak past, she brushes off all that has happened with a casual remark: 'Forget it… let's not talk about anything.' She reads my eyes and knows well that I am going through similar emotions of sadness.

Her early days in Mumbai were fraught with challenges very different from those she faced in the village. Father was ailing and I was almost two years old. We lived in a chawl in Malad, a suburb that was not as urbanely developed. A chawl is a building with several tenements belonging to different families who share a common toilet. It was an ordinary structure without basic amenities such as electricity and water connections. We used oil lamps and shared common water supplied through borewells.

Mother recounts that when my father went to work, she would tie me to a drum and step out to buy groceries. I was a naughty child, habitually dunking myself into the barrel of stored water; she feared that I may fall inside. When my father passed away, I was three and my little sister was one. My mother returned to the village, only to be deserted by our family. It became exceedingly difficult for a single mother to meet our everyday needs. As babies, my sister was barely clothed and I had just a thin loin cloth covering my body.

The sight of uncovered bodies offended the elders in my uncle's house. They didn't miss out on a single opportunity to insult us when guests visited; they never gave a thought to our penniless state. They could have provided us with clothes, just as other children in the house had benefitted from their largesse. Even street urchins in Mumbai are treated better, they get food and clothes. Mother's eyes still well up with tears when she recalls such poignant memories.

Mother's obvious naivety in dealing with people and her inability to cope made her struggles doubly hard. She felt cheated when Uncle Govind deprived us of our share in the inherited land belonging to my father, taking away the proceeds. I assured her that I was capable of earning a lot more than the land he had sold. I told her then: 'Let them take away whatever they want. Do not feel bad. I will buy land, property and everything that you want from my earnings. I am willing to work hard.'

When I was in school, Mother says, I completely dreaded losing her. Out of fear, I would hold her close, tugging at her saree pallu (the part of the saree draped over the shoulder). I had seen a classmate crying desperately in school. Later, our teachers told us that the boy's mother had passed away. Given my history and mental state after losing my father and sister, I feared that I would lose my mother too.

I was born to my parents after seven years of their marriage. Before my birth, our family members accused my mother of being infertile. Mother, in her innocence, would try to reason out with them that since her husband was staying away and never visited her, it was impossible to get pregnant. After their wedding, my father lived alone in Mumbai because he could not afford accommodation for two persons. Steep travel costs constrained my father's visits to our home in Mangalore; Mother felt his absence over long stretches of time.

All along, relatives took the liberty of taunting her and poking fun at her when she was staying alone in the village. While I was away in Mumbai and later in Doha, they would fill her with frightful stories about me, implying that I had deserted her forever. I took the initiative to work in the Gulf because she was keen that I work overseas for a few years. She had not anticipated being terrorised by people around her and the accompanying loneliness. Even government officials at the Public Distribution System (PDS) office denied sanctioning her a ration card after relatives gave them misleading information about her. She would be at a loss for words while explaining to them a genuine need for subsidised food grains.

Unable to deal with the tension and depression, she would pour cold water on herself to calm down. She contemplated ending her life many times. Thankfully, she could never succeed.

Throughout my childhood and young days, I saw my mother slogging all day, constantly preoccupied with a huge workload. Household chores, kitchen work, manually grinding coconut paste, drawing water from the well, watering trees, especially coconut and jackfruit, and stitching clothes—all these activities kept her busy.

Most South Indian cooking rituals involve grinding. We grind soaked rice for making dosa and idli, and fresh coconut for chutney and curries. Out of sheer necessity, Mother had to buy a second-hand grinding stone. This appliance was chipped, broken and burnt at the edges. We obviously could not afford anything better. It served the purpose and we had to make do with it.

Owing to all her hardships, my mother remained extremely weak and perennially looked frail and tired. She had dark spots on her face—the result of some sort of skin pigmentation following a lack of nutrition and constant stress.

To date, she is thankful to her sister Ratna, whom she is very attached to, and who helped her in times of distress by paying a fee of ₹5 so that my mother could learn stitching from a tutor. The amount appears awfully measly now, but in the village way back in the sixties, it held huge value. Besides, the monetary help went a long way because after learning to sew, my mother joined a stitching unit and began to earn a small salary. My aunt's son Krishna, whom I have written about in other chapters, is my childhood buddy and cousin with whom I share a close bond.

Later, in 1989, my mother joined me for the opening of my first salon in Thane. She would cook for the staff boys, all of whom hailed from villages near Mangalore. She would treat all of us to some specialties from our region, such as *banal adde* and *saradde*, preparations made of beaten rice, spiced and seasoned with mustard and curry leaves.

When I think of my childhood, I recollect her cooking my favourite dal, seasoned with curry leaves, mustard seeds and red chillies. While she cooked, the delicious aroma filled the house and I would head straight to the kitchen. Nowadays, she prepares delicacies on rare occasions.

She enjoys visiting foreign countries, but her fascination for the Gulf countries remains. She has visited Kuwait, Africa and the Netherlands. Today, she stays in the comfort of luxury, amidst the security of a family and happiness from her grandchildren, who enjoy playing around her. She looks most cheerful while playing with my son Rohil and daughter Aaradhya.

One of Mother's favourite activities is watching television serials aired on Kannada channels. Her involvement in the storyline is intense. When she narrates sequences to me, she shows tremendous sympathy for good characters and worries over the manner in which bad characters play out.

I listen to her patiently, explaining that the cast is only acting out plots and scenes written by soap writers. That they are fictitious stories meant to entertain people, and that it is pointless to stress over issues that have no bearing in her life. In response, she smiles back.

However, most of what I say about TV soaps makes no sense to her because she is a very simple person at heart. In her life, she has met nice people and she has met many villainous characters too. As a result, she subconsciously relates those personal experiences with the good and bad portrayals she sees on television. However, she enjoys watching comedies too.

Besides being an avid fan of television soaps, she is keen on attending traditional plays like the Yakshagana, a hugely popular theatre recital in Karnataka. A night-long dramatic narration of ancient Indian texts performed with exaggerated expressions along with a group of musicians, it has participants wearing colourful clothes and massive headgear while dancing and enacting scenes. She also likes to watch Tulu theatre and enjoys attending devotional recitals.

I trust that everything happens for a reason, even when we're not wise enough to see it.

—*Oprah Winfrey, host of The Oprah Winfrey Show*

chapter twelve

THE CHEERFUL GIRL WHO MADE A PLACE IN EVERYONE'S HEART

RIP Harinakshi (4 December 1973–10 March 2008)

The wooden boat stayed afloat in the holy Ganges at Benares. It was an unusually calm day. Harinakshi's ashes were scattered alongside chrysanthemum flowers bobbing on the smooth bed of the water. The priest who performed the religious rites on the embankment gave me some more flowers and petals to immerse in the water. That was the last I saw of Harinakshi, flowing in tranquility in the sacred river, as the gentle waves took her away, far away, to a beautiful place. A place that knows no agony... no sorrow... no pain. Only peace and happiness.

✂

We were betrothed in the year 1993 and bound in matrimony six months later in a grand traditional wedding conducted with Hindu ceremonies. We were blissfully married for fourteen years.

Harinakshi came into my life like a breath of fresh air. Serene and charming, she was the epitome of happiness, a relative term albeit appropriate to describe her for the cheer she spread around. Her infectious, lively personality made me learn what it meant to be truly happy.

I would never on my own have known how to savour the little things in life. Maybe there had been no one thus far with whom I could share life's beautiful moments. With Harinakshi, even the rough and tumble of everyday rigour seemed delightful.

She is a very nice girl. She would make an excellent companion for you.

Words could never have been truer. A friend, Anand Bhandary, from Kinnegoli village near Mangalore, said this about Harinakshi, while playing matchmaker. When I heard that she was working as a cook, my heart melted. I agreed to meet her immediately.

Harinakshi, hailing from Daregudde village, worked as a cook at the house of Anand's relatives, who were also her local guardians in the city. The couple, Anant and Rukmini Bhandary, worked at the multinational Larsen & Toubro, and were known to Harinakshi's family.

I wanted to marry a simple and down-to-earth girl. Harinakshi, I thought, would relate to my simple background and empathise with my hard times.

I had been anxious about our meeting as I rode pillion on the motorbike with my friend Somshekar Bhandary, who was acquainted with the couple. Somshekar, then a steward in Mumbai, is now a media person owning an established tabloid in Bangalore.

A plain-looking lady invited us into the apartment as I rang the doorbell. I knew in an instant—she had to be Harinakshi. We were welcomed by Rukmini, who made us comfortable, chatting about the weather and issues concerning our community with Somshekar, who was also a social worker.

That our visit was a pretext to introduce Harinakshi to me was told to Rukmini only later. Meanwhile, Harinakshi spent most of her time in the kitchen. She offered us tea and biscuits.

Wearing a long, loose cotton garment, a blend between a maxi and a nightgown, slightly torn at the shoulder and her hair tied in a braid, she looked humble and unpretentious. Sentimental about our first meeting, Harinakshi kept this garment, in its torn state, securely folded in the cupboard as a remembrance until her end.

Her simplicity impressed me. I liked her sweet smile. Her charming demeanour will stay in my mind forever.

Discussing the possibility of a marriage alliance, we gathered that her family was very poor and lived in a dilapidated house in Daregudde village. Unable to afford an electricity connection for the house, they made do with kerosene lamps at dusk and twigs to light the kitchen fire. In the monsoons, rainwater poured down the broken roof covering made of coconut palms.

Harinakshi was the second of three siblings. Her father, addicted to alcohol, had a small barber shop by the roadside. Her poverty-stricken background made me feel even closer to her. I had already made up my mind. I did not commit though, for I had to take my mother into confidence about my decision. I had to inform Uncle Sanjeev, who was introducing me to several prospective girls from wealthy families, all of whom I had vehemently refused.

Naturally, he did not approve of the alliance with Harinakshi. It did not matter as my mother was supportive.

An informal engagement ceremony at home followed, in the presence of both our families, including her parents—father Appu and her mother Ratna Bhandary. I gifted her a grand saree, a gold ring and jasmine flowers for the betrothal.

We soon began talking over the phone; we usually chatted after her guardians left for work. I would call from a phone booth because in those days, landline connections were difficult to get, the waiting list was lengthy and mobiles were non-existent. I gave her my neighbour's phone number to call on in case of an emergency; otherwise, calls were made by me so as to not burden her with bills to pay.

Our next meeting was at my new salon in Mulund; she came along with Anant while it was still being refurbished. Daintily dressed in a green cotton saree, wearing jasmine flowers in her hair, she looked very beautiful.

Exchanging smiles, we greeted each other. An unspoken bond had already been established between us.

In a while, we managed to steal a few moments to talk to each other. I asked her how she was and enquired about her family in the village. Our exchange lasted a few minutes. Before taking leave, she gifted a tiny card, hand-made by her, with 'Good Luck' written on it and flowers drawn at the corners. I was floored.

The next day, I thanked her for visiting. We spoke at length about anything and everything, and many sweet nothings. All we wanted was an excuse to speak. Our romance blossomed.

On Saturday and Sunday we became two restless souls. I felt awkward about calling when Anant and Rukmini were at home, during weekends. Their holidays were like long, empty spells. We longed for a new week to begin and we longed for Monday to dawn soon.

After some days, I yearned to meet her. At the same time, I felt it was improper to visit her place even though we were engaged and the wedding preparations had commenced. It was an unspoken traditional rule that a betrothal did not permit us with a license to meet without the consent of family elders; we could not cross the line of what may have seemed 'unacceptable'.

How long could I wait though? My impatience got the better of me. A few days later, I planned to drop in unannounced.

So I sped off on my bike the day her caretakers were at work, without informing her that I was on my way. When she opened the door, I did the cheesiest thing by saying that I was in the area, and so I had dropped by. In my heart, I was hoping she would infer what I really meant.

Pleased to see her, I began blushing. She caught my bluff and simply smiled. Fortunately, no occasion arose to plan a secret meeting after this one incident, with wedding preparations in full swing. We were married in March 1994. Thereafter, we got to know each other better during our honeymoon, when we travelled south to scenic spots such as Ooty and Conoor, and visited historical spots in Mysore and Bangalore.

A school dropout, Harinakshi had studied up to Class Seven in the village school, unlike me. I was a Class Five student when I quit schooling. Being artistically inclined, she pursued a career in beauty and hair care after a short stint at a parlour in Thane. She was an excellent cook who could put together a range of traditional Mangalorean cuisine in a short span of time. She also enjoyed singing melodious bhajans (devotional songs) and decorating the doorway with rangoli (patterns made with white and coloured sand powder) each morning, and she always dressed immaculately in cotton sarees.

Her favourite songs were popular Kannada dedications to Hindu deities: '*Kapadu Shree Satya Narayana... Narayana Satya Narayana...*' and '*Gajamukha Ganapati Vandana...*', the latter paying obeisance to Lord Ganesh.

Every morning, Harinakshi would be up early, bathe, offer prayers and hum tunes while watering plants growing on the windowsill of our flat. She liked to nurture flowers and aloe vera. The morning prayer ritual would consist of lighting a traditional oil lamp that would be placed at the foot of the tulsi (Indian basil) plant. The house had begun to feel like a home. Her vivacious energy spread cheer in the household.

Harinakshi was particularly keen about celebrating birthdays and anniversaries. Before her presence in my life, my birthdays came and went, feeling like any other day. Back then, I was unmindful of their significance. I would even forget the day.

For the first time, after our wedding, it felt good to celebrate with my favourite sweet payasam (rice pudding) prepared by Harinakshi. She gifted me a wallet, arranged money notes in an orderly manner inside and showed me how to use it. Until then, I used to hurriedly stuff money into my pocket.

I gave her a surprise gift—a gold necklace—on 4 December that year, her first birthday after our wedding. Her joy knew no bounds. She liked wearing trinkets of jewellery. We hosted a small party at the salon, she cut the birthday cake and the staff sang and danced for her.

Our staff respected her immensely for a simple reason: everyone was equal in her eyes. If a pair of slippers was bought for one member of the staff, then a similar pair would be purchased for the rest. On our weekly holiday, Monday, she would plan picnics to the beach, cook a special lunch for them at our home or surprise them with ice cream treats at work.

She was an extremely friendly person who took pleasure in entertaining people, participated in community activities and took up considerable social work. She held a special fondness for an orphanage at Airoli in Navi Mumbai, often visiting the children there with gifts and donating money for their projects. From her, I learnt benevolence and how to help the needy.

After two years of marriage, we purchased the shop adjacent to our Mulund salon to start an exclusive section for women. Ever since she began working, our clientele increased. I believe that Harinakshi brought a lot of luck and prosperity. Our salons prospered, and they still do with her blessings.

As a couple, we seemed well-matched, with our thought processes flowing in the same vein. There were times when she would spell out my thoughts even before I could speak my mind and at other times, I would read her mind out loud. Mystifying, yet fascinating, that two hearts were entwined in one soul. At times, it did baffle me, but in a very nice sense. I felt the adage 'made for each other' was for real and suited us the best.

Since she liked to groom herself, I liked to do up her hair, style it and even cut it.

She fondly called me Putta, which meant little baby, and I called her Ammi, which meant baby girl. Often she would tease me lovingly: '*Nanna putta tumba tunta* (My baby is very naughty)'.

Harinakshi was very keen to become a mother. For nearly two years, she underwent treatment under the renowned gynaecologist, IVF (In Vitro Fertilisation) and fertility specialist Dr Indira Hinduja, hoping to have a test-tube baby. The treatment involved taking regular injections for which she took it upon herself to travel alone from our home in north Mulund to the hospital at Mahim, towards south Mumbai. Owing to my busy schedule at the salon, she travelled alone. Somehow, the treatment never helped her.

As time passed, I noticed that she was falling ill quite often. She would be unwell over long periods. We consulted a doctor in the area who suggested undergoing a laparoscopy. However, the doctor, we understood much later, had not sent the results for testing and had arbitrarily prescribed medicines saying she had tuberculosis (TB). At that point, we believed him.

For a year and a half, she was swallowing tablets to cure TB, an ailment she did not even have. When we realised that her condition was not getting any better despite medication, we consulted another gynaecologist and obstetrician, Dr Sangeetha Shetty in Mulund, who informed us that TB was a wrong diagnosis. We had to stop those medicines immediately. Dr Shetty informed us that although the laparoscopy had been carried out, the sample was never tested to find out the real problem.

We felt terribly cheated. 'How would the doctor know she

had TB if the sample was never tested?' she demanded of us and we were at a loss for words.

Dr Shetty had a hunch that Harinakshi's ailment was a far more serious problem and hence she put us through to the most respected oncologist in the city for further consultation—Dr Sultan Pradhan at the Prince Aly Khan Hospital. Tests revealed that she had several fibroids in the uterus and they were multiplying at a fast pace.

She was immediately operated upon—it was her first surgery in 1999. We were under the impression that after the removal of her fibroids, she would be on the road to recovery. We did not imagine her condition would worsen. I was in for a shock after being told that Harinakshi was suffering from cervical cancer.

In a private talk with the doctor, we decided against informing Harinakshi about the ailment, at least for some time, hoping she would show signs of recovery with medicines. I was not prepared to break the unfortunate news to her. I knew she would be shattered to hear about the diagnosis. Most of all, I could never see her sad or in pain.

The next step was to pay attention to Harinakshi's diet to increase her immunity levels and general fitness. Dr Venu Nair, naturopathy practitioner, altered our diet by including healthy foods and put us on a yoga programme. I am saying 'we' because I joined Harinakshi in following the diet that included fruits such as red grapes for its antioxidant properties and to increase the haemoglobin count in the blood.

We would consume juices made out of dudhi or bottle gourd and wheat grass cultivated in our home on the windowpanes. The new diet and exercises helped my health. My excessive worrying eased, breathing exercises made me a lot calmer and my hair stopped graying. Harinakshi felt a little better, but that hardly made a difference to her overall health.

Two years after the first surgery that involved removing the fibroids, she had to undergo a second one as the new ones were growing faster. This time, the doctors had to remove her uterus much against her wishes. The decision was extremely painful, for she was longing to have a child. But the doctors were adamant as the fibroids were continuing to reproduce; they were unstoppable.

It was an awfully sad day for Harinakshi. She did not imagine the seriousness of the situation during the initial stages, nor did I imagine that life would come to such a pass. She was in a state of shock when the uterus was taken out.

Now, I thought, was the time to let her parents know about her worsening health condition. Until then they had been kept in the dark. They were aware that she was unwell, but clueless about the seriousness of the situation. In one's old age, it is difficult to bear sadness. Eventually I gathered enough courage to reveal her real state. They were heartbroken and miserable. All of us were shaken and depressed. Somehow, in that hour of crisis, I felt that I had somebody to share my sorrow with. So far I had hidden my grief from Harinakshi and my mother by putting up a brave show in front of them.

Her father, who was addicted to alcohol, had given up drinking totally on Harinakshi's insistence. Five years after we got married, when Harinakshi was in good health, she had organised a traditional rite called Kola, which she believed would rid her father of his dependence on alcohol. Kola is an ancient practice of spirit worship that people in Mangalore and surrounding towns and villages have been following over ages with abiding faith. It is an expensive, elaborate, night-long dance recital to appease the spirits, believed to be local gods or guardians of the village. Harinakshi made her father take a vow at the ritual and once a promise is made here, it is never to be broken. Ever since, her father abstained from alcohol.

Even I had to give up alcohol after Harinakshi began to

think that my drinking was owing to depression caused by her illness. She thought I was drowning my sorrows by gulping down whisky. I would share a few pegs with some staff members or drink alone. I asked her not to feel bad and assured her that my drinking alcohol was not on account of the reason she imagined but due to fatigue.

However, to make her happy, I told her that if she felt responsible for my drinking, then I would stop having alcohol. She replied with a single word of caution: '*Please*'. Promptly, I stopped.

Some months later, her condition began to deteriorate as the infection had spread inside the body. The doctors decided to operate for the third time, after which she had to undergo chemotherapy. After her third operation, doctors advised me to fulfill any wishes she may have had.

She had very little time left, they told me. I could not believe what I had heard. I could not accept the fact that she was seriously ill, that she would leave me and all of us, sometime soon.

Her condition had degenerated to such an extent that the food pipe had twisted, resulting in her inability to swallow food. She would throw up all that she ate. Yet, I did not reveal the seriousness of the situation to her. I hoped for a miracle cure because she was devoutly religious, reposing supreme faith in God.

She remained under a cloud, until one day, she read the label on a bottle as medication for cancer. She was completely devastated. She stared me in the face, stunned, too terrified to speak. I saw the ghastly fear in her eyes. I myself was at a loss for words, dumbfounded.

What could I say? That I was willing to try out any treatment to cure her of the ailment? She was already aware that I would go to any lengths to seek every cure possible. She knew that I was willing to do anything and everything just for her sake.

Deep inside me, I could feel anger simmering. I was livid with my own self for sounding terribly shallow. It was a situation that was not within my control. I felt so helpless that I was devoid of options to alleviate her pain.

I could only say that I was always there for her.

Taking the doctor's words seriously, within a week, we were sightseeing in Singapore and Malaysia with the help of a local club that organises group tours. Enlivening the experience were many couples and families, all part of the tour. Walking about merrily as though nothing had happened, eating delicacies to her heart's content, Harinakshi enjoyed the stay, laughing, talking with everyone and shopping happily.

Nobody would have guessed that this was the same person on a hospital bed the previous week, with pipes stuffed into her nose and machines monitoring her health. To our surprise, she recuperated fast. That was how she was, extremely strong in her mind and determined to get well soon. She was fighting the disease with an unflinching quest to live, fully aware of its seriousness.

Six months later, in 2005, we decided to visit the UK to learn advanced courses in hairstyling at premier institutes in Central London. We stayed in the UK for about fifty-five days. I joined the well-known beauty and care specialists, TONI&GUY, while she joined Vidal Sassoon, the place where I had completed my earlier course.

While studying, we stayed with the same family that had been my host earlier when I was in London for my course—Purshottam Sota, his wife Kumudben, their sons Rahul and Ashik, and daughter Priya with her husband Bhavesh Kotak. Harinakshi mingled effortlessly with the family, cooking south Indian dishes such as neer dosa and coconut chutney in their kitchen. Their meals, mainly Gujarati dishes, were vastly different in taste, yet they relished her south Indian fare.

Harinakshi's exuberance was overwhelming. Nobody would have guessed that she had undergone operations or that doctors had given up on her condition only a few months ago. Our hosts, aware of her illness, never discussed it with her, but they would express their anguish and shock to me.

I completed my course in a week while she took about a fortnight. The rest of the days were spent visiting castles, museums, parks, meadows and enjoying rides on the hop-on-hop-off buses in London. She thoroughly enjoyed the slight drizzle that would come down ever so often when we stepped out. She took to the weather comfortably during the English summer when flowers were in full bloom and fresh morning dew glowed on them. She particularly enjoyed watching cows grazing in the countryside. She would take photos of picture-perfect scenes, houses and flowerbeds on pavements. Pleasure walks through parks and green fields filled her with energy and gave her boundless joy.

While walking through the shopping arcades, she liked to choose fabrics with floral prints. 'They are just like this beautiful country,' she would say. She was fascinated by the underground tube service and one day in our enthusiasm, we lost our way. We laughed at our stupidity and began to traverse the distance, slowly realising that it would take a good amount of time to cover the stretch until we found our way to a more familiar place. That is a day I cannot forget because it was the first time she showed signs of tiredness. It was my fault, actually. I was confused about the roads leading to our host's place.

Despite doctors saying she would live for about two months, she went on for another two years. It was sheer determination and will power that pulled her through the illness. Her resilience was commendable. Despite a tormented body, her mind desired to be active. Back in Mumbai, she continued with her daily activities, managing the salon, cooking and conducting daily prayers. She even began to contemplate adopting a child from the orphanage she visited at Airoli. Remarkably, all through her illness, she kept up a smiling face.

But chemotherapy's debilitating effects had begun to show. Her lustrous, long and healthy hair had started falling drastically. Like dry weeds clinging to an old, unattended brick wall, her hair too seemed to lose its hold and came off in clumps. Both of us went through severe, indescribable trauma.

Harinakshi was a brave woman. She was not one to give up. Tying a cloth over the head to cover the sparse hair, she would tell clients and friends, when they enquired, that she had returned from the well-known Tirupati temple in Andhra Pradesh, where devotees shave their heads, offering prayers in return for the fulfilment of their wishes.

But after she underwent her fourth operation, her work came to a complete standstill. After all, how long could she endure the excruciating pain? I felt helpless even as I tried to calm her down. Moving in and out of hospitals and between many CT (Computed Tomography) scans and laparoscopy tests, she had to go through chemotherapy a total of sixteen times!

She would say that she felt as if insects were crawling within her body, biting into her and gnawing at her insides, and at other times, it felt like someone was poking with a sharp pin all over her stomach. While sleeping on the bed, she experienced sensations of pinching or someone twisting her skin and flesh. These torturous spells of biting, pricking and pinching happened every now and then, and as a consequence, she could not sleep a wink at night.

Hence, I resorted to keeping her mind occupied. I told her some fictional tales to divert her attention. I would talk sweetly in her ears to soothe her mind, so that her fears and the accompanying stress wouldn't augment her aches. Often, I felt like crying along with her. I may not have experienced her pain physically, but I was sensitive enough to feel it. If I broke down, I was sure that she too would weep with me. So I put up a façade of composure.

Meanwhile, many of our friends and clients came to know of her illness. We could not keep it under wraps for long. One of our clients told us about an ayurvedic practitioner called Deobappa, who stayed near the temple town of Trimbakeshwar in Nashik, about 160 kilometres from Mumbai. The healer, who had a considerable number of patients seeking medication, said that we had approached him when Harinakshi's illness had reached its last stage, and therefore he could not give an assurance of curing her.

His medicine consisted of the bark of a tree, which had to be boiled in water, and Harinakshi had to drink that concoction. Whenever her situation got bad, I would drive down immediately to Deobappa and collect the herbs for fresh medicines. In a span of nine months, I travelled to the place forty-seven times, with Harinakshi accompanying me at least fifteen times. It was our last attempt at saving her life. Many times, I had to cancel my appointments with clients, speed off at night and return the next morning to Mumbai without wasting time.

Travelling to Nashik would tire me out. I would look exhausted owing to lack of sleep. My clients would ask me what was troubling me. Had the tension driven me into seeking respite in alcohol or drugs? My eyes had turned bloodshot, my skin had become dehydrated and my health had started to wear out. Physically, I looked completely worn out. But there were so many people who had been cured by Deobappa despite being extremely unwell. That instilled some hope in me for Harinakshi.

Nobody wants to die. Everyone wants to live. Besides, Harinakshi was still so young.

In desperation, we were willing to try out everything—therapies, alternative medicine, superstitious beliefs and 'godmen' who proclaimed to cure. Another person told us about a spiritual man known as Patharwallah Baba, which literally meant 'Godman of Stones'. He was so named because he could talk about the ailment and the extent of the illness simply by placing a stone on the patient's palm and offering herbs as medication. This time, the remedy did help in easing the pain. But signs of recuperation or even some progress in her health seemed bleak.

Obviously, it began to affect her well-being. There were days when she would feel extremely low and depressed, perhaps it worried her that she was left with very little time. She got involved in doing more social work by donating generously to temples and social welfare groups. She devoted considerable time to praying, especially when she was downcast, and refused to meet clients at the salon.

In the last three years of her life, she put her heart and soul in seeing her dream home, named Durga Nilaya, being built at Daregudde village. Harinakshi's presence is conspicuous; a smiling photo that hangs on the wall of the drawing room welcomes anyone entering the abode. There are several items in the house that evoke her memory, as all of them—utensils in the kitchen, upholstery in the drawing room and the tiles in the bathroom—were personally selected and purchased by her.

Some of her belongings are still there, namely, her sarees, all in vibrant colours, hang in the wardrobe just as she had arranged them. It was a home that she had longed to live in for many, many years. If that was not to be, then I believe at least the home décor articles which she had bought so lovingly should continue to be there for as long as possible.

10 March 2008

That morning, I was feeling down and edgy after seeing Harinakshi's agony. I was compelled to attend to a court matter in South Mumbai. Harinakshi was complaining of a sharp and piercing pain that was becoming increasingly unbearable. Our lawyer advised that my presence was important, and so I decided to leave for the court, much against my wishes. I did not feel like leaving her side at all.

Harinakshi was lying on the bed. She looked feeble, very weak. While I was saying bye to her, she patted my cheeks, like she always did. In that debilitating state too, she was feeling bad for me, since I was caught up with legal issues.

'You have a lot of tension because of me. And now this case... You are troubled with so many problems.'

She ran her frail, trembling fingers along my face and told me to take care. As I was leaving home at around 8.20 a.m., I assured her that I would return home in the afternoon.

Midway to the court, I received a call on my phone. Raghu (Raghav Bhandary), who has been working for me for many years, informed me that Harinakshi's condition was deteriorating and that I should hurry back. The pain was getting severe. She was screaming loudly and calling for help. Her parents, my mother, some family members and the salon's staff were already beside her bed.

Her eyes were rolling back in their sockets, and she was flapping her legs and arms—signs of her body losing all sense of control and muscle movement. The doctor was called in to check her condition and immediately she was taken in an ambulance to a nearby hospital. But those were her last moments. She passed away around 11 a.m. on 10 March 2008. She was thirty-five years old.

Dr Manish Motwane, the general physician who was with her during her last hours, said that she had breathed her last in our home. I was inside the court premises when a relative called to tell me that her soul had left her body. I turned ice cold. I could not react.

Two days before her death, due to severe recurring pain, she had been admitted to the hospital on Dr Motwane's advice. Unable to eat, she had been administered glucose.

She had become extremely thin and her bones showed quite prominently. Even in a state of acute illness, her hair had grown out beautifully, sometime after chemotherapy was stopped. Her overall condition was worsening. When people came to visit she could hardly speak, she was losing her ability to interact. I was aware that she was gradually sinking.

In the court premises, my hands and legs started shaking after I heard that she was no more. Everything around me seemed to be collapsing. I could no longer stand steadily on my feet. My friend Vinod Chopra, who had come with me to the court, helped me sit down on a bench in the vicinity. Someone gave me a bottle of water to drink. I tried to say something. I could not speak. My voice choked as I was beginning to suffocate.

We did not wait to take my car, which was parked some distance away from the court. I was helped into a cab so I could rush home. Everything around me felt numb and frozen in time.

I could feel the traffic moving beside our cab, but not the cacophony of wheels and honking vehicles which are commonplace on Mumbai's roads. Our cab driver was asking me something; he turned to look at me and made gestures, yet I could not hear a word of what he said. So shocked was I that I became stone deaf to the world.

Deep inside me, I always hoped that my Harinakshi would recover someday. That she would never leave me. She often said that she hated the idea of my living alone after she would be gone.

Subconsciously, one part of me was not willing to accept that she would die, although I was aware of the harsh reality of her health, of the cruel fact that she would be with me only for a short time. The doctors had been keeping me updated on her deteriorating health. And another part of me had been preparing for this eventuality. But honestly, one is never prepared for something like death.

Until that moment, I had really believed that she would live long.

In the cab, I was a broken mass of confused emotions. After a brief period of numbness on hearing the news, I began to feel remorseful, and gradually an unapologetic anger set in. I was angry, outright livid that she had left me. As the cab neared home, I could see a huge crowd assembled in our building premises. Wails of mourning engulfed the apartment. Harinakshi's parents, her family members, my mother, relatives, friends and clients had gathered in our apartment. I tried to compose myself as I entered the house.

Looking at the body, I could not believe that only a few hours ago, I had spoken to her. Now, there she was on the floor, resting quietly. I tried to pat her cheeks to wake her up. Would she not respond to me? I sat there gazing at her. In those few moments, I thought, she was finally relieved of agony and distressful pain.

The ritual of bathing the body and dressing it in a colourful saree is customarily carried out for a woman who passes away while still married, as opposed to practices followed for a widow's death. I requested those conducting the ceremony to let the gold chain with a heart-shaped locket remain on her body during the cremation. She was immensely attached to this necklace; it was a gift that I had given her soon after we got married. As per her wish, we also kept a tiny string of black beads taken from her mangalsutra, the black-beaded chain worn by Hindu married women, on her body.

At dusk, after 7.30 p.m., she was cremated at the electric crematorium and her ashes were immersed in the holy waters at Trimbakeshwar, near Nashik, and then in the Ganges at

Benares, in Uttar Pradesh. With that, I felt that a huge part of me, my soulmate, my closest companion, had gone away forever.

Time and again Harinakshi would say to me, 'You have cared for me like a parent would for a child.'

I do wonder if there are more couples like us; if there are, I can say with confidence that they are a rarity. We were two people of one mind.

Life without her was devastatingly lonely. I no longer wanted to go to work; yet at home, I felt agitated. When people visited to express their condolences, I would never let them leave me. I felt the need to have everyone around. Friends kept reassuring me that I had cared for her and nursed her very well through the illness.

Her absence was all too evident everywhere I went. When I went out into the terrace, I could hear her calling out to me, but when I turned around, all that greeted me was an empty space. In the prayer area, her presence was strongly felt because that was the place where she would spend the most amount of time.

Since she loved children, I hosted a lunch for the students of her school at Daregudde village.

As the Hindu saying goes: She was like the goddess of wealth, Laxmi, stepping into my home, bringing in prosperity and changing my life for the better. I remember her smiling face the most. I also remember the way she laughed—loudly, without a care in the world. She was full of life. Everyone teased her with a nickname—Tunti—which means mischievous. With her exuberance, her positive approach and selfless concern for everyone, Harinakshi had etched a permanent place in everyone's heart.

Dream is not what you see in sleep; it is the thing that doesn't let you sleep.

—A.P.J. Abdul Kalam, missile scientist and former president of India

chapter thirteen

COURSES, CERTIFICATES AND ACCOLADES

Hairdressing Courses Studied in England

- Creative Course—a Diploma at Vidal Sassoon Academy in London, 1998
- Advanced Cutting and Technical Course—a Diploma at TONI&GUY Education Academy in London, 2005

Awards and Felicitations

- Won the first prize at the Wild and Wacky Hairshow Contest held by Salon International. Trophy awarded by Christopher Mann, Chairman, Fellowship of British Hairdressing, and Commissioner, Salon International, 1998.
- Shri Guru Prasadita Yakgalana Mandali—Vishveshvaraya Sabha Bhavana, Matunga Karnataka Sangha, 2001
- Felicitated in recognition of achievements and contribution to society—Mulund Royals, Lions Club, Mumbai, 2010
- Felicitated with the Pinnakles Award for holistic contribution towards styling traditions and crafting trends in the glamour world—All India Hair Barber's Association (AIHBA), Maharashtra chapter
- Received the India Book of Records certificate for Shiva's

Hair Designers Pvt. Ltd. for organising the 'Biggest Hair Colouring Marathon'. About 1,511 people were participants who had their hair coloured in 12 hours at Chitrakoot Grounds, Andheri, Mumbai, in 2011. Godrej Industries was associated with the event.

- Nominated for Asian Top Fashion Hair Stylist of the Year at Fashion Asia 2011, China
- Bestowed with Bhandary Kula Ratna by the World Bhandary Federation, 2011
- Presented with the International Hair Designer Award by Bhandary Seva Samiti, Mumbai (part of the Kachhuru Shree Nageshwar Temple, Barkur, Udupi District) during the Kachhuru Utsav, 2011
- Felicitated with Samaj Ratna for redefining and uplifting the community's profession (Kula Kasbu) and for outstanding contribution to society—Bhandari Seva Samiti, Mumbai, at the Annual Family Festival, 2011
- Felicitated by the Kulala Sangha, Mumbai's socio-economic committee, during the Kulala Dance Festival, 2012
- Felicitated by Sahitya Balaga, Mumbai, 2012
- Awarded the Sanman Patra by the Udupi Taluka Savita Samaj. Honoured for contribution towards Kannadigas in Mumbai and for being the pride of Karnataka—Karnataka Sangha, Goregaon, Mumbai
- Awarded Samaj Ratna—Salon Beauty Parlour Association, Maharashtra, 2013
- Felicitated for achievements—Presidency School, Mahaveer Foundation, 2013-14
- Felicitated by Kateel Durgaparmeshwari Prasadita Dashavatar Yakshangana Mandal, 2014
- Felicitated for contribution towards the Tulu community living outside Mangalore and for bringing international fame to the Tulu community by excelling in the art of

hairdressing—Kalasamsada, Mumbai, of the Akhil Bharata Tulu Oakuta, Bright Awards Night, 2014

- Felicitated by Karnataka Janapada Parishath—Kerala Gadinada Ghataka, Kasargod, Kumbale, Bangalore, 2014
- Received Karnataka Award—Abbaka TV, 2014
- Honoured by Kannadiga Patrakara Sangha, Maharashtra, 11 April 2015
- Honoured at the 11th World Kannada Cultural Convention, Toronto, Canada, 27-28 June 2015
- Felicitated for outstanding support for the skill development programme of MANAS. The award was presented by Dr Najma A. Heptulla (Hon'ble Union Minister, Govt of India), Shri Devendra Fadnavis (Hon'ble Chief Minister of Maharashtra), Shri Dinesh Singh Bist (Joint Secretary, Govt of India and Founder Chairman of MANAS)—Bunta Sangha, Kurla, Mumbai, 4 September 2015
- Presented the Rashtriya Vikas Ratan Award (for M/S Shiva's Hair Designer Pvt. Ltd.)—Economic Growth Society of India, Delhi, 12 September 2015
- Felicitated by Ryan International Group of Institutions, 7 January 2016
- Awarded Popular Unisex Salon Chain of the Year in the category of Times Retail Icons 2016—Times Group, 9 March 2016
- Felicitated for becoming a successful businessman in his field of work—Celebrating the True Icons, Society Icon Awards 2016, Magna Publishing Co. Ltd., Mumbai
- Felicitated for outstanding contribution towards furthering policies and schemes of the Ministry of Minority Affairs for the welfare of minority communities by Dr Najma A. Heptulla (Hon'ble Union Minister for Minority Affairs, Govt of India) under the aegis of MANAS, at Vigyan Bhavan in New Delhi, 28 May 2016

- Felicitated as Bollywood's Hairstylist Supremo and on completion of thirty successful years in the beauty and hair care business by *Stardust* magazine, a Magna Publication. In May 2018, the special Stardust Initiative issue, dedicated solely to Shiva, showcased his incredible achievements and rise to the top.
- On 14 June 2018, *Stardust* celebrated the grand success of the issue at an event attended by well-known personalities from Bollywood, business, industry and media. Shiva was hugely applauded for setting up a chain of nearly twenty salons in Mumbai and for his future plans to open many more in the city.
- Felicitated as the Grooming Expert of the Year at the Times Power Men 2018 by The Times of India Group in Mumbai
- Awarded with the Most Innovative Hairstylist of the Year by the Global Leaders Awards, UAE. The award is given to those who promote entrepreneurship and small business at the international, national and regional level.
- Conferred the European Entrepreneurial Professional Knowledge Doctorate Title by European Continental University, 9 May 2015

Share your knowledge. It's a way to achieve immortality.

—His Holiness the 14th Dalai Lama,

Tibetan spiritual leader who works toward promoting world peace chapter fourteen

TUTORING YOUNG STYLISTS

> Presented to Shivarama K. Bhandary in recognition of his outstanding contribution for furthering policies and schemes of the Ministry of Minority Affairs for the welfare of Minority Communities
>
> —thus reads the plaque handed over by Dr Najma A. Heptulla, Former Union Minister for Minority Affairs, Government of India, on 28 May 2016, at Vigyan Bhavan

I was felicitated for conducting courses in collaboration with the Government of India's Ministry of Minority Affairs and MT Educare, a leading tutorial business venture under the aegis of MANAS (Maulana Azad National Academy for Skills). We had our first batch of nearly 150 students, aged between sixteen and twenty years, in February 2015. Girl students belonging to minority communities enrol themselves for a certificate course on beauty and hairstyling taught free of cost at Shiva's Training Academy in Andheri.

Four trained students, two employed at Shiva's and two others who have set up their own businesses, were invited by MANAS to speak at Vigyan Bhavan about their experience and the benefits of taking the course.

Receiving the felicitation was one of the most memorable days of my life. The occasion filled me with a sense of tremendous satisfaction and I felt honoured to have shared the front row with luminaries from the field of sports, beauty and arts. Several lawmakers, who were seated behind us, were applauding our achievements.

Shiva's Training Academy was started in 2010 as a regular training centre conducting courses through the year. Back then, students were coached in beauty and hair care modules held in collaboration with L'Oreal, the leading cosmetic brand worldwide. From 2015 onwards, the training programmes, which run to full capacity, have been held in association with MANAS. Students are trained under our talented and creative staff who groom top filmstars and celebrities in Mumbai.

In the first batch of the training programme by MANAS, we had several girl students, many of whom were in Class Ten. They would juggle between the course and school studies during the preparatory leave before their final exams in March. With most of them hailing from economically backward sections, students attending the course, even today, include young mothers who come along with their babies because there is nobody to take care of them back home. There are young girls shouldering responsibilities at home; they complete household chores in the morning to be free to attend the course late in the afternoon.

In 2015, Dr Najma Heptulla and Maharashtra Chief Minister Devendra Fadnavis similarly felicitated Shiva's Training Academy, and me, when students were sanctioned loans to start their own businesses, albeit small, after undergoing the course. There is surely a certain amount of personal fulfilment in educating young talent and empowering them with employable skills that can be put to benefit.

Many students have shown remarkable enterprise and promise in pursuing a career in the field. Some have taken old furniture from Shiva's salons to set up shops; some others have purchased used chairs and mirrors from elsewhere. A few secured loans from Axis Bank, a facility provided to them by MANAS, to start a venture from a rented premise or from their homes. A few others have chosen to provide door-to-door services. They visit people's homes to attend to their beauty needs.

At the academy, the curriculum includes training students in all aspects of hair care, styles and cuts; the area of beauty care comprises make-up for a range of occasions that could vary from specialised make-up for brides, parties, day events, photoshoots and the like. The syllabus teaches the latest trends in skin care, manicure, pedicure, waxing, applying mehendi (henna) designs on the hands and feet and the use of lotions and cosmetics.

The students are also tutored in the knowhow of various tools such as scissors and combs; it is important to learn how to choose the best kit from an assortment available in the market, and understand the one that suits each individual while working. Students are given hands-on practical experience in handling hair dryers, hair-straightening gadgets, togs and other coiffeur's equipment correctly.

One of the main teachers at the course, Melissa D'costa, who trained in a Mumbai salon accredited to CIDESCO, the well-known international institution for beauty and spa therapy, has formulated a special curriculum for the entire course, dividing the session between theory and practical work. Raghav Bhandary, head of operations, and Shweta Bhandary, technical head, along with other top stylists and hairdressers at Shiva's, oversee the smooth functioning of the courses by devising session modules and maintaining regular interactions between trainers and students.

When D'costa, for example, teaches threading procedures, she demonstrates the process that involves entwining the thread around the fingers to pull out unwanted hair to shape eyebrows.

Then she explains different skin textures and the consequent skin reaction that may occur in case a threading process is not conducted properly or goes haywire. She explains how to handle the thread tenderly so as to not cause harm or scar the sensitive areas above the eye.

There are longer sessions on the subjects of haircuts and hairstyles with live demonstrations by top stylists from Shiva's. A staff member or a friend stands in as a model on whom demos are conducted to explain every little detail about giving the right haircut in the simplest manner. Students try their hands on the model's hair under our careful observation. I advise them to try giving haircuts to their family members or neighbours, for additional practice and expertise.

Often, I stress that if they are able to cut and style the shortest hair growth of about less than a quarter inch in length, then it could be concluded that they have mastered the art.

I show them how to hold the comb and the scissors when handling very short hair by displaying the technique on a model. I hold the comb facing upwards and snip the hair jutting out of the fine teeth. This is the method I have been following throughout my career to cut and shape minuscule hair growth, and in my experience, it is the most comfortable technique and the easiest to follow for any hairdresser. It appears to be as simple as running a comb over a wee bit of hair, but in reality, perfecting the technique and becoming proficient at it requires a great deal of practice and deftness. By following this method of snipping, however, a hairstylist can be sure of never injuring a client's scalp.

For instance, in earlier times, only an experienced barber used an old manual clipper to sweep off tiny hair follicles from the nape after a haircut. Now, the electric or battery-operated gadgets are the easiest and safest. I demonstrate with an electrical clipper to students and show them how to adjust the degree of speed before using it on the model's neck. Every step requires detailed explanations and every gadget is shown to students like it were a rare exhibit. We have to bear in mind that such everyday tools are new and sophisticated for young pupils whose exposure is limited, despite living in an urban environment.

At the same time, I brief them about old tools by putting out on display my collection of barber's implements. A worn-out hairbrush that has lost most of its bristles is exhibited on the table with a mixed bag of tools that look equally archaic. An old pair of scissors made out of iron, heavier than the modern ones, gleams as it is regularly polished with kerosene oil to keep rust at bay. There is a barber's knife and a shaving blade, a leather strip to sharpen and chisel the knife's edge after every three uses, and a bottle with a long tube to pump water out, akin to a spray bottle!

At the outset, students look confused, euphemistically speaking, studying the war-weary armour. After watching the use of modern gadgets, they cannot imagine how a barber ran a salon working with what looks like antiquated apparatus. These tools are very dear to me and hold a special place in my life; it was with their help that I learned my craft, honed my skills and perfected my art. Without them, I would never be where I am today. Someday, I plan to display the tools in a fitting manner in a special showcase.

During the course, I show the video of the Silver Jubilee celebrations of Shiva's salons and some media interviews published in newspapers and aired on television.

I tell them that when I started out as an apprentice at a barber's salon, customers were hesitant to take my services since I was very young and inexperienced in their opinion. I had to impress clients with my skills until they began to trust me with the work.

My voice still chokes and I feel a lump in my throat whenever I speak about my days of struggle during the course. Gradually, however, I am able to get back to the present and continue narrating my life story. Despite all the progress I have made in life, despite being in a position of authority to do the things I like to do and despite being able to buy all that I ever wanted to in my young life, remembering my childhood still brings tears to my eyes.

I try to hold them back. I feel like there is a bundle of emotional knots stuck in my gullet. I feel numb for a few seconds. I try to swallow the pain, but it takes a while. I drink some water and then try to speak again.

For those few seconds, my mind traces those hard and painful days once more. It feels like I am experiencing those horrible incidents all over again. Does pain really ever go away completely from our mind, our subconscious? It does not seem so. I try to compose myself. I manage to say something hesitantly, as though I am carefully picking up each jagged piece of a shattered glass pane. I begin to narrate the key twists and turns of my life and describe the fallout of every tragedy.

This occurs quite often as I recount my scrambled childhood filled with setbacks and sorrows. My talk happens at the end of the training session when students are mentally preparing to wind up for the day. In between controlled yawns and sighs, sleepyheads try to stay upright when I begin.

Then, as my story unfolds, the students begin to listen. I tell them about this very poor and uneducated boy who struggles and suffers in pain. They begin to look at me with rapt attention and their interest begins to grow. I inform them that braving all odds, I worked all day and late into the night with undying perseverance to achieve my goals.

At this point, usually, they start empathising with my story since most of them are from poor families. I feel it is very important to let them know about my struggles, because I hope that they will derive some inspiration from my story.

Perhaps my talk has nothing to do with the curriculum of a beauty and hairstyling course. But there are many lessons to learn. Students need to know that in life, they may experience several setbacks and pitfalls and nothing is going to come easy to them. They will face obstacles, jeers, competition and they may not do well at the outset. Most come from humble families, many are in their late teens, many are breadwinners for their families and many others are looking for avenues to earn income. They must keep the faith and focus on their objective. They have to learn that hard work and honesty, two key elements of success, will take them far in their career.

When students come to the academy, they are dazzled by the glamorous setup, top-class facilities and the latest products on view. They begin to wonder how I could have acquired all the paraphernalia exhibited on the walls and in the showcases—the mannequins, electronic gadgets, huge mirrors, high-end cosmetics and lotions required for beauty treatments. The ambience creates a surreal feel. For them, it is a place out of a fairyland where goodies are waiting to be grabbed.

Many students may have spotted beauty and hair care tools in magazines or perhaps in shops. However, they have never ever had the opportunity to even touch them. Therefore, the eagerness to learn, use and handle the equipment all by themselves is awe-inspiring. The excitement is palpable, even infectious.

They giggle, smile, chat and make noise. There is a certain childlike innocent quality in young minds. These youngsters are yet to step out into the big real world of the beauty industry and experience its challenges. For the moment, they are taken in by the sheer range of styles and fashions and the art of make-up. At the bridal session, the academy lights up in a festival-like atmosphere. Students enthusiastically bring borrowed bridal clothes and traditionally designed ornaments and animatedly form groups. One among them becomes a model-bride for the session and the rest gather around her. Someone applies make-up on her face, another dresses her up in the wedding attire and yet another helps add to her look with the jewellery. After that, they pose for selfies with their smart phones and request the rest of the staff for a photo session. The picture becomes a keepsake.

What is heartening is that some classes are so visually enriching that they inspire girls to make small videos accompanied by a musical soundtrack, which they send to me on WhatsApp. It includes my talk, video clips of ramp walks and hairstyles, particularly the one held at the group's Silver Jubilee celebrations in 2013. Everyone is keen to learn bold and wacky hairstyles, showcased in the video, created by a team of hairdressers at Shiva's. For that, they would have to wait until the next stage of learning in an advanced course. To reach the second stage, they would require a certain amount of practice to wield the comb and scissors confidently without hurting or injuring clients.

I tell them that the more they practise, the better skilled they will become. At least six months of working in a salon is necessary before they start with advanced training. I even counsel that if they fail to get a job at a salon immediately they should opt to work without pay since, at this stage, learning and working on clients is of primary importance. In the process, there is a possibility that they may understand their area of preference—specialising in any of the areas of beauty, haircutting, spa, drawing mehendi, tattoo or nail art. There are innumerable options in this sector. Students must show dedication and willingness to work hard. Then the world will be their oyster.

To love someone is to understand each other, laugh together, smile with your heart and trust one another.

—*Unknown*

chapter fifteen

A LOVING MOTHER AND A PATIENT WIFE

Each day, now, I zip through a series of non-stop activities—meandering through traffic, visiting my salons, attending to exclusive clients, meetings with the staff, training students, checking with new products' suppliers, keeping appointments with specialists from the beauty and hair care industry and catching up with other sundry work.

After what seems like a tiring day, to be home gives me a huge sense of relief. It's the warmth of a home that I look forward to, as my car heads to our apartment in a multistoried building. All credit for making my home into a caring abode goes to Anushree, my wife, whom I married after Harinakshi passed away.

Anushree is a compassionate person. Patience is a wonderful quality in her. She is a loving and responsible mother to our children, Rohil and Aaradhya. She cares for my ageing mother and attends to her needs. In her, I have found a suitable partner to share my life with, someone who empathises with my struggles.

She helped me overcome the tragedy of losing Harinakshi and pulled me out of gloom. Anushree has brought happiness in our lives. There is a feeling of contentment within me because of her.

When we met for the first time in the household where she was working as a caretaker and cook, she appeared to treat our meeting like another chore to be completed. She looked nervous, though. My friend Vinod Chopra came along with me and we exchanged pleasantries with the family.

Several suitors had gone to her employers, Mrs Rekha and Mr Ramchandra Nayak, who own a flourishing business named Karaya Traders at Uppinnangadi, a small trading and religious centre about fifty-five kilometres from Mangalore, with proposals for Anushree's hand in marriage. However, none of them showed genuine interest. All turned her down after the first meeting itself.

Obviously, to her I was yet another among the many suitors who had come to ask for her hand. She was sure I would refuse. She thought to herself, of all men, why would *this* man accept my proposal? In her view, I was a good-looking, well-settled businessman who owned several salons in the country's financial capital. She, on the other hand, thought of herself as a poor, simple-looking girl who was working in a household since teenage. Besides, she had only studied up to Class Six. *Why on earth would a well-established man from Mumbai want to marry someone like me*, she had thought, and asked me later about it.

At the outset, I was reluctant to marry again after the passing away of Harinakshi. I refused to meet many prospective girls whose photographs my mother would show me. I was still in mourning and missing Harinakshi's presence in my life. I was trying to put this sorrow behind me by throwing myself deep into work. I would leave at the break of dawn and return very late in the night, juggling between three outlets at Thane, Mulund and Lokhandwala.

There was a buzz in our community about my being single, and since Harinakshi and I had no kids, I was considered an eligible bachelor too. However, my mother and Harinakshi's parents wanted me to move on in life and remarry.

Anushree's proposal came to me through a cousin, Krishna, a tenant of Mr Nayak, who was asked to follow up with me after Ms Rekha's ageing parents had noticed Harinakshi's obituary in the local papers. Soon after, the Nayak family met me at a wedding that I was compelled to attend in Karkala, since the bride was related to Harinakshi. Before she passed away, Harinakshi had bought a gold necklace to gift to the bride hoping to be present at the event. Hence, my presence at the occasion was important.

At the wedding, I informed Krishna that persuading me to meet someone would prove to be a futile attempt. Accordingly, he gave the message to Mrs Nayak's parents and I thought the matter had ended there, but I was wrong. The pressure to remarry began to mount, with my mother persistently dissuading me from living a lonely life. Affluent families from within the community tried luring me by offering me shop space to set up more salons. They must have assumed that I would be pleased to accept their daughter's hand if it helped me expand my business.

Then my mother and Harinakshi's mother came up with a canon of a tradition followed among Hindus. When there is a death in the family, the household must have a wedding event within the year of the passing away of a person, otherwise as per the tenet, a wedding could take place only three years later. My mother insisted that three years was too long a waiting period. Each day, she would push me into thinking about remarrying. 'How long would I be there for you as family?' she would reason.

Finally, I agreed to meet Anushree, only because she came from a humble background, which I believed would give her the maturity to understand my struggles. I could not imagine marrying a girl from a wealthy family who had rich tastes. I thought that I might have to alter my way of living. What if I had to take her pet dogs for a walk each evening? Basically, I am a simpleton at heart.

In our first meeting, Anushree asked me why I would want to marry her. I explained to her that Harinakshi, my wife who had passed away, was also a very simple person who, at one time, had worked as a cook in a Mumbai household. I was clear, however, that I was not looking for Harinakshi in another person; she occupied a special place in my life and the woman I would marry would have her own place in my life as well. I would not compare either of them because I respect that each one has her own personality and individuality earned by her own right. That made sense to her, and she understood my keenness to meet her with a proposal to marry.

Later, when I decided to marry her, Anushree again wanted to know the reasons for choosing to take her as my life partner when many others had rejected her earlier. Her suspicions were justified. In her place, anybody would have doubts. After meeting her, I realised that we were similar in many ways. Like me, she had quit school to help manage a family of six siblings; they could hardly subsist on her father's small salon in the village. Her simplicity, straightforwardness and down-to-earth approach appealed to me. During this meeting too, Anushree was cordial; however, she did not even smile while speaking to me.

She took me to visit her family who lived in a ramshackle house at a short distance from the Nayak residence. We took the dirt mud road from the backyard, walking through an uneven passage, dodging thorny bushes, avoiding stones and pebbles. Leading the way, she would continually turn around to caution me about the small obstacles in our way. I would smile at her innocence.

Today I may be sporting the best brand of shoes; however, these very feet have trodden rough paths umpteen times. She was unaware of my tough past. It was obvious that she was uncomfortable about her poor and unkempt house. I was offered a chair in the courtyard and tender coconut water to drink. For me, the meeting was only a matter of courtesy. It was not going to influence my decision. I had already made up my mind. The wonderful meal cooked by her—she is an expert and enjoys trying out different cuisines—impressed me more than I had imagined possible!

Funnily enough, when I first met her, she had been confused—wondering who among the two men (Vinod and I) had actually come with the proposal. She told me much later, after we got married, that to her, we looked quite like goondas or thugs in our casual wear—expensive T-shirts, sneakers, sunglasses and driving a fancy car—like the garish-looking gangsters portrayed in South Indian films.

Her employer, Mrs Nayak, and her parents had done a background check on me, and Anushree had blindly followed their advice. I asked them to watch *Zindagi Live* on IBN7, a Hindi television channel, to give them a better idea about my background. It was a show about successful people that was being aired at the time; and the team had interviewed my mother and me, and featured my life story, my struggles and my achievements.

Rekha had described Anushree as a simple, diligent, caring girl who also assisted in keeping a check on money matters in the business. She was more of a foster mother to Gauri, Rekha's daughter, whom she had cared for since she was a child. Gauri, a dentist, is now a close confidante who gives tips to Anushree on fashion and food.

Anushree and I were married on 27 February 2009 in a traditional ceremony attended by relatives, friends and staffers at the Laxmi Devi Kalyan Mantapa, Karkala. It was a daylong event consisting of an engagement ceremony in the morning and the wedding ritual at noon. Anushree's original name was Lalitha, and my mother suggested we name her Anushree, another name of Goddess Laxmi.

Thereafter, Anushree and I got to know each other better while spending a few days in Goa and Mumbai, and then we left for Dubai on a short holiday. Her initial days in a new home and a new city were filled with anxiety and fear. For someone who had not seen the world beyond the little town of Uppinnangadi and thereabouts, the cosmopolitan life in Mumbai was a culture shock. Apart from tall buildings, crowded streets and packed shopping malls, she had to learn to adjust with urban habits, an eclectic crowd at the salons and the frequent visits of staff members to our home. Shweta, Raghu's wife, a beautician at the salon for fourteen years and a relative of Harinakshi's, was Anushree's sisterly support and guide during the initial period.

The first time I saw a big smile on her face was in Dubai, when we went on a safari. Each time the vehicle went over a sand slope, she would giggle and give a full-throated laugh. Finally, she seemed to be opening up, I thought, beaming to myself. We visited the Burj Khalifa, the fish aquarium, relished eating in the open desert tents and enjoyed boating in the creek. At the gold souk, I bought her a pair of fancy danglers, besides taking her shopping for cosmetics and bags.

But now she has comfortably settled at home and adapted herself to the urban life, be it socialising or attending to guests. Mumbai, in her view, is a city that provides numerous possibilities to people, and to women in particular. Girls are empowered, enjoy freedom and know how to make independent choices. The city is lit up late in the night, girls move out alone and nobody finds that odd. Small towns, on the other hand, have little to offer to girls who have to abide by stringent practices and norms.

Anushree enjoys shopping and feels at ease in both Western and Indian wear. She likes to pick up trousers, jeans, tracksuits and trendy tops. I encourage her to wear watches as I am fond of them. She follows a beauty regimen; she colours her hair and styles it on special occasions.

She has long chats on the phone with Gauri; they share a commonality of views on fashion and home decor. Gauri, on her part, feels that Anushree's life is a fairytale, just like Cinderella's. Her Prince Charming has swept her off her feet and taken her to stay in a palatial house. To me, she is a loving wife, and to our children, a responsible mother. She is also an exceptional cook, whose preparations I look forward to eating once I'm home. Most times, I am unable to be at the dining table with my family, but the food is packed in tiffin boxes so that meals are not skipped.

However, she does object to my alcohol binges in my hometown at Daregudde, the only place where I drink without a worry. She tries to dissuade me; I do understand her concern and lessen my intake.

What I appreciate most about her is that she never complains about anything. My work hours are erratic, I return home late each day, sometimes after 11 p.m. or even 1 a.m., depending on the rush at the salons. Travel takes up time because of distances and traffic snarls, particularly while visiting salons at Dombivili in the far north or at Chowpatty in the south of Mumbai. She never protests that I am not there with our children to help them with their studies, or to drop them to school or accompany them on other outings. When I do find the time to be with our children, I usually enjoy their pranks, join in the noise and savour the mischief-mongering.

When the kids are at school, Anushree visits the Lokhandwala and Juhu salons. She has good business acumen and managerial skills and understands how to administer efficiently. She also handles money matters well, understands the latest fashion trends, and has the required capability to evaluate employee performance.

There have been occasions when I have erringly called her Harini—short for Harinakshi—the name I would usually call my first wife to seek her attention. At such times, my mother has yelled at me if she is within earshot. My old staff feel stunned whenever this happens in front of them, but they understand that I can make a mistake because it is an old habit. Of course, I make quick amends and call out her name immediately after.

Anushree, however, would look at me and laugh. She would come up to me and ask what I need, never feeling offended. She takes it all in her stride. That is the extent of her calm disposition. She displays a mature understanding in any situation.

Personally, she does feel settled in life and prays that it continues to remain like this. For someone who thought that she would never get married, this change has brought a sense of contentment. When she was single and suitors were rejecting her, she had plans to adopt a girl child and have a small home of her own. Her employers, the Nayak family, were on the lookout for a house until I entered the picture.

She says that her wish to have a baby girl was fulfilled after Aaradhya's birth. She enjoys buying clothes and dressing her up, and if there is a fancy dress competition in her school, then Anushree is busy as a bee, experimenting with dolling her up in different avatars. If the school demands that Aaradhya has to be a horse or a giraffe in a stage act, then her mother is out in the market, hunting for the right attire.

When Anushree was pregnant the first time, she had a craving for bananas. We were surprised that she was eating them because she dislikes the fruit. My mother, who savours them, would quip that it was a sign of things to come. The first-born would be a boy because she longed for a grandson. Anushree, on her part, wanted a girl, so we chose the colour pink to shop for clothes, toys, baby paraphernalia, including the paint for the room. And I wanted a healthy baby—a little bundle of joy. But, as is commonly believed—*Mother knows best, listen to her.*

On 16 September 2010, Rohil was born. The doctor called me in to see the newborn soon after he was given a wash. I felt overwhelmed. My joy knew no bounds.

After a little over twenty minutes, the doctor came out with the baby wrapped in cloth. The black mop of hair on the head was the first thing I noticed as the doctor handed him over, placing him gently in my arms. He was making cute sounds and wriggling about in his tiny frame. After a while, the three of us—Anushree, baby Rohil and I—were in the room together.

Later, Shweta took our pictures on the mobile phone. In a while, the nurse took the baby away and Anushree was told to take rest. But my excitement was only growing. I sent the picture to family members, close friends and our staff through WhatsApp and distributed sweets to everyone.

Like my mother, Rohil, or Rolu as I fondly call him, is a soft-natured boy. Aaradhya, lovingly called Aaru, born on 2 July 2013, is a tomboy. She hits her brother and bullies him. In return, he smiles back, and does not even retaliate. I like that quality about him. He takes care of her, protects her. When I see the two playing, I imagine that my sister and I would have played in a similar manner. I was very protective of my baby sister too.

Since I have missed out on a lot in my life, I feel tempted to indulge my kids with toys, clothes and little treats. But I do so within my limits. Every moment spent with them is precious.

On Sundays, I take Rohil with me to play tennis at a nearby club. On our return, like two playful boys, we bathe, have breakfast and get ready to go to the salon. Aaradhya, three years younger to Rohil, is usually asleep then.

The reason I take Rohil to the salon is for him to know about his father's occupation. When I tell him that his daddy works hard, he is full of questions, wanting to know the meaning of 'hard work'. I learnt my craft at a very young age, but I would not like to force my son to do the same.

Both Rohil and Aaradhya share the same excitement to use the newest hair products that come to our salons.

Rohil's hair is cut short as per school rules. He likes to make spikes on top of his head by doing a touch-up using water as a medium. In the salon, he has seen adults using gel to style their hair. Aaradhya, like all little girls, is fascinated with new clothes and new hairdos. As for Anushree, well, she goes with what is latest on the fashion scene—long hair with curls, multi-layered mix, 'U'-shaped long layers and sometimes braids with flowers.

The true sign of intelligence is not knowledge but imagination.

—Albert Einstein, genius scientist

chapter sixteen

FROM SILVER TO GREEN, YELLOW, PINK... WAITING FOR THE GOLDEN

A handsome young lad came to the Juhu salon for a haircut in early 2013. As he waited for his turn, I noticed that he had an attractive face and a reasonably well-built body. I overheard him chatting animatedly with one of our staff members about workouts and the nuances of building a good physique. Later, while I was styling his hair, giving him spikes on the top, finely tapering it on either side and running a long straight line with a razor on one side—a style I conceived at that moment—I saw his face glow. He was extremely excited with the new look.

Right then, I had an idea. I asked him if he was keen to model on the ramp with a fancy hairdo at Shiva's Silver Jubilee celebrations, scheduled to happen at the end of the year. From then on, he became a regular at the salon, asking me to give him the same style. Eventually, owing to personal commitments, he could not participate in the event, although his sister and father did attend the function.

The incident is important because this is when it struck me that in eight months' time, Shiva's would be completing twenty-five years in the business. I got cracking on the idea of having an exclusive presentation. I thought it was time to thank all the people who had stood by me, wishing me well, guiding and advising me, and simply being there to gently correct me on issues regarding work and business.

With our target of 7 December 2013, my team at Shiva's, my associates and friends started planning the nitty-gritty of putting up a gala event. We wanted a grand show; it was to be a celebration of not just the achievements of Shiva's salons, but also a commemoration of a coiffeur's profession and the hairstyling industry overall.

While planning our strategies, we worked on two categories: one featuring a broad range of styles from the 1960s to 2010, and another set from 2011 onwards up to 2025s futuristic designs. For that, we had thirty models, both Indians and foreigners, modelling forty-two hairstyles for the show.

We put our best foot forward to showcase different eras to demonstrate a wide-range of collection in hair fashion that has been in vogue. Travelling nearly fifty years back in time, we put up a splendid display of fashion, ranging from the retro and the flower power days of the '60s followed by the swinging '70s, the panache of the '80s and the chic forms of the '90s. We tried to mix the new-age elegance of the twenty-first century with contemporary tastes. Adding to that, there was an entire decade foretelling future styles, going hand-in-hand with a slew of eclectic designs, on display at the venue.

I took inspiration from the fairytale character Rapunzel, known to cascade her long hair down the tower, so that her Prince Charming could climb up to the cellar where she had been locked up by a witch. Finally, on the day of the event, when Rapunzel-like models flaunting long braids and hair flowing down to their feet, nearly sweeping the floor, opened the event on the runway, there was a momentary hush, as the attendees gasped in awe. A split second later, they were all cheering, clapping and whistling.

All at once, I felt a bit nervous and a tad happy too, but I could not express myself. I clasped my hands tight, as I had goose bumps all over. I could not see the hair on my arms rise, since I was wearing a formal coat. I felt my cheeks flush.

I have always had a fascination for the long hair sported by most traditional Indian women, their braids swinging down to their waists. I have had many opportunities to style Indian brides in a variety of braids on their wedding; hence, the quintessential long plait had to be the opening on the ramp.

The Christmas tree-inspired hairdo, replete with decorations, in keeping with the festive Yuletide season in December, drew a lot of attention. A svelte model in a red evening gown sashayed down the ramp with a huge conical hairstyle; it was made of curls and rolls that fell out like the branches of a fir tree, with tiny dangling festoons. The whacky style sent the audience into raptures.

Each model wore a distinct look. A bevy of tall and slender girls, some wearing red, black and white evening gowns, some in mini skirts, a few in leather shorts and others in chiffon sarees, posed in ultra-glamorous hairdos. They sported sleek updos, double buns, a mix of perms and layered cuts, frizzy hair, beehive twists, French braids twirled into buns and pigtails, fringe bangs, shaggy waves, side hair rolls stretching out as if a magnet were pulling them and ringlets made to stream on bare, tattooed shoulders.

Feather plumes, flowers, beads, ribbons, elastic, bands, nets and clips—a dazzling assortment of enhancements added chutzpah. Blonde, burgundy and copper-coloured highlights shimmered in the arc lights.

The gang of boys dressed in smart, casual and grunge attires presented a mix of elegant and outlandish styles. Looking rugged and edgy, they took to the ramp with pizzazz, showing off braids, cornrows, Afro, Mohawk, crop, punk and the eponymous ponytail with twists and curls. Streaks of silver grey, blue and gold highlights glistened in the men's hair.

The peace symbol depicted on the back of one model's head was a tribute to the international award I had received for the same theme in the early days of my career.

Futuristic styles were aglow with fluorescent shades—burgundy, cobalt blue, forest green, flaming orange and shocking pink. Sporting neat and simple hairdos of straight, waist-length hair in monochrome and psychedelic colours, models portrayed a new, snazzy flair.

The kaleidoscopic colour range that was being introduced on the global fashion scene is now a craze. Clients are experimenting with bold colours and moving ahead from the time when they preferred to tint streaks compatible with their original hair colour. Two months prior to the event, I had demonstrated an assortment of hairstyles on a dummy at Shiva's Academy to train my staff to be able to assist me without any glitches on the day of the gala. I set aside two days per week to train them in a range of hairdos, besides teaching them to blend the styles of Bollywood and Hollywood movies, to discern between day and party wear, and to recognise casual and corporate trends. I prepared them to handle backstage work so that they would be proficient enough to do a quick touch-up on models once they had completed round one and were getting ready for a second lap on the ramp.

The success of the event squarely goes to the dedication and hard work of my staff—nearly thirty people, who have now become like my second family. I am immensely thankful to fashion house L'Oreal's support and for bringing out a coffee table book on my creative hair designs. And I am grateful to my 'business friend' Rajiv O. Khandelwal, who ideated on several counts such as models, stage, backdrop and camera work, and filmed a documentary on me, which was then presented at the event.

The celebration gave me an opportunity to reveal my skills in cutting and styling a model's hair in several layers in a matter of four minutes. Someday, I would like to demonstrate this feat in two minutes.

What made the occasion even more special is the camaraderie among my guests, Bollywood celebrities and other prominent personalities hailing from different walks of life. I could feel that there was a sense of togetherness and a shared bonding usually seen in close-knit families. My immediate family was there too, looking happy and enjoying every moment of the event.

My mother was gleaming with pride and satisfaction, while my wife was affectionately smiling with a sense of contentment at my success. As for my children, my son kept himself busy, playing pranks around the hall of the five-star Taj Land's End, Bandra, where the event was held, and my daughter, hardly a few months old then, was blissfully asleep most of the time, not knowing what the matter was. Someday, when they are old enough to understand my journey, my children will see the pictures of the show and perhaps rejoice in sharing my achievement.

Several people at the event said they could not remember another fashion show of hairdos put up on such a grand scale. I felt overwhelmed and humbled at the same time. I always feel that there is a greater force, perhaps spiritual, which is leading and showing me the way through all the twists and turns of life. There are people close to me, many of them my clients, who have directly or indirectly influenced me, guided me and been a vital part of the success. Many of them took time out from their schedules simply to be there to share my success. And I am truly grateful to them.

Some of them joined me on the stage, including filmmaker

Madhur Bhandarkar, film producer Sunil Lulla and his wife Krishika Lulla, actors Neil Nitin Mukesh, Mugdha Godse, Anjan Shrivastav and Raju Kher, dance choreographer Sandip Soparkar and model Neha Hinge. I continue to thank them and wish them bountiful happiness, prosperity, love from their near and dear ones and above all, God's blessings.

They spoke eloquently about my friendship and my success. Film directors Abbas-Mastan said they felt the event was like a family programme and not a commercial show. When it was my turn to speak, I was tongue-tied. At such times, words just do not come out of my mouth! I wanted to say so much, to pour out my heart, my feelings, my happiness, my misgivings and my fears, but the enormity of the occasion was such that I could barely utter a few words. I thanked everyone present for coming and making the day so special. I wish I had said more... it was indeed a once-in-a-lifetime occasion. I tried to hold back my emotions as I spoke to the media, who were attending in large numbers and have always been there to encourage my work through the years. Whenever I have attempted to display a creative design based on the popular topic of the time, the media has enthusiastically covered and also aired all my work on television and web portals.

But on that day, when news television crews were interviewing my mother, she simply could not stop sobbing. My wife and children were standing around her. 'Why are you crying?' I asked, as she wiped her moist eyes. 'Don't cry. You have been the one telling me not to cry each time I broke down. Now you are shedding tears,' I gently coaxed her.

She grew calm after that. Like me, she too was overcome with emotion, her voice choked and she could not find words to express what she felt in her heart.

Small, daily, seemingly insignificant improvements and innovations lead to staggering achievements over time.

—Robin Sharma, author and leadership guru

chapter seventeen

REACHING FOR TWINKLING STARS, SPARKLING SKIES

All through my life, my naps have defined my economic status. The places where I have snoozed or caught my forty winks mirror my life's ladder of success.

It was a childhood fascination to own a house. I would imagine that some day I would be living in my own home. Nowadays, children play house using props such as cloth, cardboard or plastic to make a tent-like structure. I used to be alone; I had no one to play with. Using bamboo sticks, I would build a playhouse in the compound, big enough to crawl into. I would squat inside on a used jute sack spread on the bare soil. The structure would be festooned with bougainvillea flowers.

At the time my mother and I were staying in a rundown, thatched rented place without floor tiles. At night, we slept on the floor, which was made of cow dung. Only the rich who owned bungalows had gleaming mosaic floors that stretched from wall to wall. However, that did not matter. I was sensitive to the fact that we were poor and tiles were not a concern. Besides, sleeping on the floor was our way of life.

Today, as I look back, I feel it was quite a feat to sleep on a straw mat on a hard and uneven floor without a pillow. The difference dawned on me only after I began experiencing better days. All the same, I can still doze off on any mattress, floor, bench or sofa. After a tiring day, sleep is all that matters. I snooze like there is no tomorrow. It has been like this since childhood—slog until the body is so tired that sleep comes easily. My early days at work were physically and mentally exhausting with Uncle's tyrannical ways and the beatings that I bore until black and blue marks showed over my skin and fatigue numbed my senses. Nobody thought of recuperation; sleep was the only remedy.

My mother fondly remembers how on several occasions, she tried to wake me up in the morning by nudging me with a stick passed through the room's grilled window. While staying at Kariminabai's rented place, I would lock the room and stretch myself out at night, oblivious to Mother's knocking at the door in the morning. Mothers harbour strange fears. Panic-stricken, she would insert a long bamboo stick through the grills of the open window, prodding me to wake me up. All I did, she narrates smilingly, was turn to the other side and continue snoring!

My initial days in Mumbai illustrate the city's housing woes as anyone without a roof over the head would encounter. Staying in Bhandup with a cousin was never easy. While working at my cousin's salon, I used to live in a tiny place with a loft, more of an attic actually, where I would sleep, squeezing for space with two other boys. All of us, hailing from the same community and same town, were related to each other either closely or distantly, and that affinity compelled us to help each other out. My cousin and his wife, owners of the space, used the wooden cot on the ground floor.

Covering a modest area of two hundred square feet, the tin roof dwelling sloped on either side like an inverted V. If we were to sit up in the loft at night, our heads would hit against the tapering roof. Bending our backs, we would cautiously slide to the centre area, where the roof was slightly higher, to huddle for a chat.

My next stay at Ramabai colony, in suburban Ghatkopar, was in a shelter near the marshy land, now a heavily reclaimed area with growing habitation. Rows of tenements built cheek-by-jowl with asbestos sheets were susceptible to rising temperatures in Mumbai's hot and humid weather. Inside hot tin walls, the place seemed like an overheated furnace roasting our bodies.

The surroundings reeked of foul odour. A stifling and repugnant environment gave me a constant headache and also a nagging toothache. The area typically characterised the city's slum pocket with open sewers, piles of unattended garbage on pathways, shelters made of tin, cloth, plastic and bamboo sticks, water scarcity problems barely resolved by roadside municipal taps and tangled electrical wire connections running in crisscross patterns. Danger lurked in every corner because bootleggers and criminals lived alongside poor families and strugglers like me.

However, for me, the biggest troublemakers in the area were the mosquitoes that buzzed around my ears, depriving me of much-needed uninterrupted sleep. Large and fierce, they stung the skin, drawing out blood like vampires. The marshy swamps in the vicinity were breeding grounds and that explained the huge clusters droning above our heads. Mosquitoes are attracted to the colour black, just as bees are to honey. They swarmed in full fury on top of my head in rapid circuitous aerial movements. I would pull the blanket over my body, face and head to avoid frontal attacks. Even today, I am particularly sensitive to mosquitoes.

My daily routine work was stressful, and hence sound sleep was necessary. Since I had to combat the mosquito menace through the night, I would try to catch a few winks early in the morning, the only time when municipal water flowed into the taps. Water was scarce, therefore I would take help from

Shiva's dream home at Daregudde village in Karnataka

Shiva with his wife Anushree, son Rohil and daughter Aaradhya

The swish interiors of Shiva's Signature Salon at Walkeshwar, Mumbai

सामना

फुलोरा

शिवा की कैंची बोलती है...!

An article titled 'Shiva Ki Kainchi Bolti Hai' in *Saamna*

Shiva receiving a doctorate from the European Continental University

Christopher Mann, Chairman, Fellowship of British Hairdressing and Commissioner, Salon International, awarding Shiva with the 1st Prize in the 'Wild & Wacky' Hairshow Contest held in Mumbai in 1998

Shiva while attending the Advanced Cutting and Technical Course at TONI&GUY Education Academy in 2005, in London

In London on a tourist hop-on/hop-off bus

Shiva training for the Creative Course at the
Vidal Sassoon Academy, London, in 1988

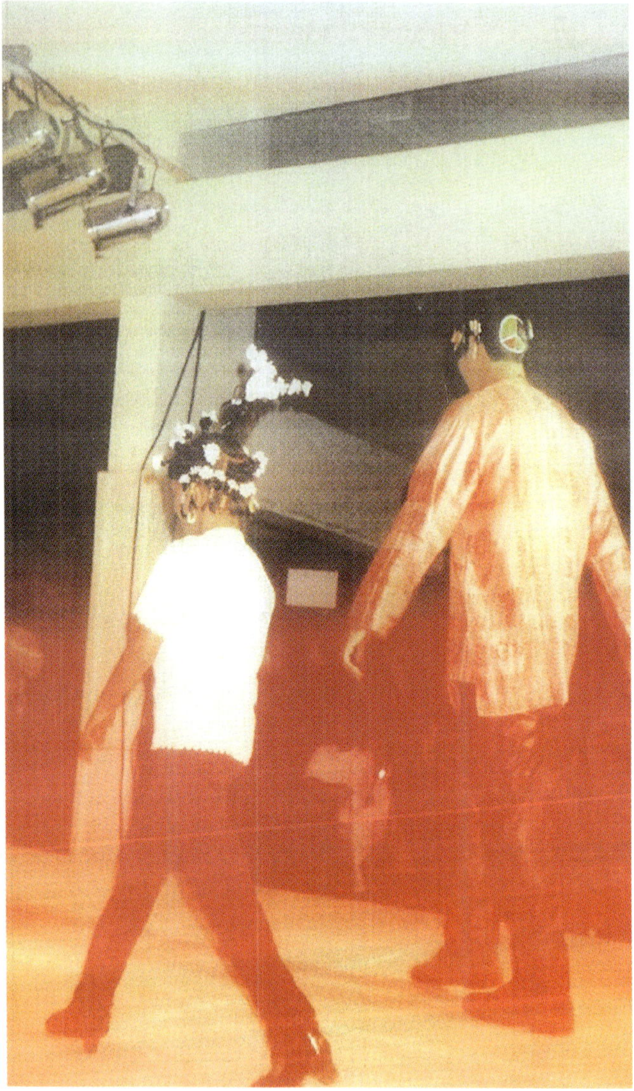

At an international hairstyle competition,
Shiva created a peace symbol on the back of a model's head
and bagged the World Peace Award

Shiva with the students at the Shiva's Training Academy

All about mentoring – Shiva with students at Shiva's Academy

Shiva with his mother, wife Anushree and son Rohil
outside the salon in Lokhandwala

Shiva with filmmaker Madhur Bhandarkar

(R-L) Actors Mugdha Godse and Neil Nitin Mukesh; filmmaker Madhur Bhandarkar; and film producers Sunil Lulla and his wife Krishika of Eros International

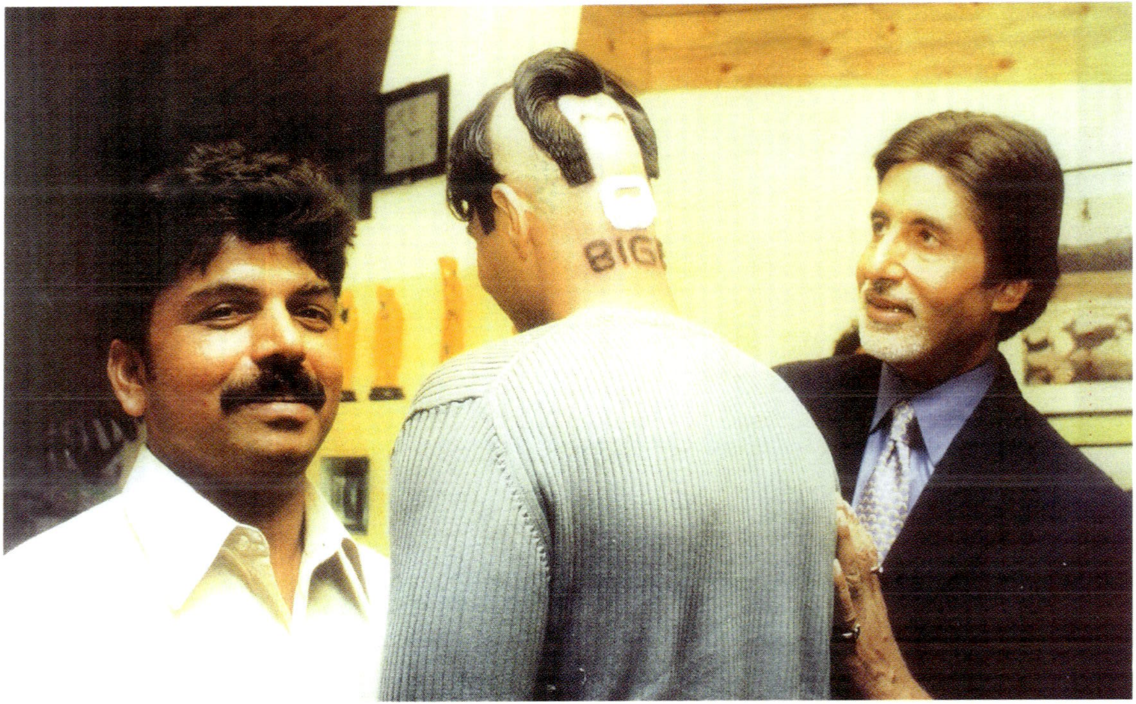

Superstar Amitabh Bachchan admires his iconic beard style, which he used to sport during one of the early seasons of the 'Kaun Banega Crorepati' television series. The style was emulated by Shiva on a client's head and shown to the legendary actor on the sets of KBC in Film City, Mumbai.

Models flaunt longish braids on the ramp at the Silver Jubilee celebration

Models applaud after putting up a splendid show of hairstyles commemorating a coiffeur's repertoire at the Silver Jubilee celebration

Shiva with the late Balasaheb Thackeray

Filmmaker Madhur Bhandarkar; Shiva; Aditya Thackeray, Shiv Sena Youth Leader, and Ashok Dhamankar, Director, Magna Publications with his wife Jayshree

Chief Minister of Maharashtra, Devendra Fadnavis
honours Shiva at the MANAS function in Mumbai

Former Minority Affairs Minister, Najma Heptulla honours
Shiva at the MANAS function in New Delhi

Press clippings from newspapers and magazines adorn the wall of one of Shiva's salons

women in the neighbourhood; they were kind enough to fill up buckets in exchange for a token amount of money, which I used to insist upon since I felt that they too were sparing time from their busy household chores to do me a favour. Despite facing severe challenges on a day-to-day basis, I preferred staying in Mumbai because I was earning enough to fill my stomach.

I narrated the story of my year-long stay at this squalid colony to Suresh Anna (Bhandary), a prominent person in our community and a successful businessman. We were at the wedding of Dinesh, Rukmini and Anand Bhandary's son, the couple with whom I had stayed in their asbestos dwelling. He was shaken, to say the least, even though he knew of my appalling past. I share past experiences with Suresh Anna because he too had to wrestle through tough times since childhood. I feel he empathises and understands. At Bhandary community meetings, he talks about my success story as a fitting example to be emulated, to enthuse the public.

Sometimes, I feel dazed reflecting on these past incidents. I am struck with wonder at my own resilience in overcoming many dreadful phases in my life and retaining my sanity through it all. At least now I am able to smile about it.

After Ghatkopar, I had to return to Bhandup to work in my cousin's salon and sleep in the loft. For want of sufficient air to breathe, as opposed to sleeping in an atmosphere of mugginess, I opted for the open premises of a wayside temple, alternating that with the corridors of a school on the opposite side. Gentle winds blowing across the leafy green campus relaxed my tired bones. During the monsoons, however, I was left with little choice but to scamper to the loft.

I left for Doha hoping to see better days, but my living conditions worsened. I was in for a rude shock about my work, which was gruelling and demanding. I went as a barber to work in a salon that was being built in an upcoming games stadium.

Since the arena was not ready, my employers assigned me the work of carrying bricks on my head and sacks of cement on my shoulder at a construction site. I became a manual labourer for a short time. But since the prospect of working in a posh salon was still open, and I wanted to give it my best shot, I refrained from complaining.

The weather would swing from extremes, turning either too hot or too cold, owing to unpredictable desert winds. In a cramped and scarcely ventilated room, there were many bunker beds but only one fan for several of us cooped up in a room, sweating profusely after a hard day's work. The conditions were not in the least bit hygienic. There was one toilet that we all shared, with only a strip covering the middle portion of the entrance—this was meant to be a makeshift door—exposing the legs of the person sitting on the pot with his pants down at the feet. It was quite a sight. Gradually, however, all of us acclimatised ourselves to the situation.

But like they say, one must always look for the good in every setback. For me, it was the first time I experienced sleeping on a proper flat bed. The bunker beds were provided by our employers, while the mattresses and sheets were arranged by us. Until then I had no idea what it felt like to sleep on a mattress, having slept on straw mats or plain cloth sheets all my life. This may not have been the best of beds; nevertheless, I understood that some comforts relaxed the body.

After a few months of drudgery, I was shifted to an under-construction stadium, where I was given a place to use as my own in a room adjoining the stadium. I started my work in a corner of the sports ground, close to the washroom, so as to get access to water while the actual salon was under construction. This time, my employers provided facilities which felt like sheer luxury—a single bed, a soft sponge mattress, a pillow, good bedsheets and covers, apart from access to washing machines.

What struck me about the Middle East was that people led a very plush life, choosing to use the best of things available in the world. I thought that there was a lot to learn from them. The newly built salon was set up in tune with international practices followed worldwide. It was a spacious place that had large chairs and huge mirrors. Excellent gadgets and the finest products were used for servicing clients. I was impressed with the way the floors were maintained in sparkling clean condition at all times.

I have implemented some of those practices at Shiva's salons. As far as my work is concerned, I have been particularly conscious of adhering to top hygiene standards in my work to the point of being finicky—cleaning shaving tools, before and after use, using new blades for every client and providing them with separate hand towels. This was even before the fear of the AIDS virus made it officially mandatory for barbers to change blades.

My days of comfort in the Middle East ended after my return to Mumbai to set up my own little salon. With a little money that I had saved up, I purchased my first shop in a 194 square foot area in Thane, then largely an industrial belt. For nearly ten months, I spent the nights on a narrow bench, waking up several times with a startle, fearing a fall. The wooden bench was only about five-and-a-half-feet long. With my five feet seven inches long horizontal frame sleeping on it, my legs were left dangling out. In the day, a straw mat covered the bench for clients to be seated on, and at night, a thin sheet served as a cover on which I slept without a pillow. In the hot weather, the front door was kept slightly ajar for air to waft in. On other days, it remained closed. The stale air inside hardly affected me since I would be dog-tired by the time the last client was attended to. Every morning, I had to rise early to use a public toilet, bathe in the salon's backyard and wash a bundle of napkins that were used on customers. A stove run on kerosene in the corner of my shop sufficed to make tea and boil eggs.

After living in this cubby hole, I rented a place comprising one room and a kitchen in a rundown building in an area called Shantinagar, mainly to have my mother stay with me. She was alone in Attur village, managing on her own, working at the cloth unit, tending to the garden yield and guarding the cultivated produce from vandals. I wanted her to be under my protective care.

As business gained some momentum, I employed two boys from our village to apprentice with me. They stayed with me while my mother looked after the house, cooking meals for us. We bought some bedding, including mattresses, bedsheets, pillows and blankets for everyone. Living together felt like we were a family.

Staying in rented places came with its own dilemmas. The landlord would evict us the very day our term ended, without bothering to discuss if an extension to stay was required. With hands resting on his hips, he would stand at the door with new tenants, while his lackeys walked in to clear our luggage and furniture. Within hours, we would be homeless. However, thankfully, it was not tough to find another place immediately. I realised that this scene would be repeated every eleven months, each time the lease period of a rented flat expired.

In 1991, finally, I bought my own house, a 2BHK apartment in a building called Shanti Vaibhav, after selling our village house at Attur and digging into my savings. Without an elevator in the building, we had to climb up four flights of stairs, but I was still content, and so was Mother. I was at peace with myself as my life was beginning to take a meaningful course.

Meanwhile, the salon was revamped with new wooden chairs and a wide mirror in place of the old second-hand furniture.

The same carpenter renovated the kitchen and crafted wooden beds and furniture for our new house. New drawers, Godrej cupboards, a music system, a television set, a divan, chairs and a showcase were set up.

Potted plants, roses and jasmine decorated the window sills. An exclusive space was given to the tulsi plant as Mother religiously prayed each morning when she lit the traditional lamp. Friends and relatives from our hometown came to visit us and were pleasantly surprised at our modest setup.

We did face power cuts and severe water crises, yet such hassles hardly mattered.

My life was gradually changing for the better—be it home or at work—and I was feeling good about it. Harinakshi had filled the void with her mirth and laughter. She was a lively person and her happiness was infectious. Our house truly felt like a home.

Our happiness was short-lived though. About five years after we got married Harinakshi's health worries had dampened her spirits and cast a shadow over our blissful marriage—her anguish to have a baby, frequent visits to doctors, subsequent revelations of a wrong diagnosis and treatment, and the eventual battle with cancer. Her condition deteriorated after the second operation as a consequence of which she was unable to climb the flight of stairs to our flat. I decided to move to another building with an elevator.

My staff members are my extended family. I feel responsible for those who do not have their own family with them in a strange city. Their struggle to find a foothold reminds me of my early days when I landed in Mumbai for the first time. Relatives gave me food and shelter and were very supportive. Despite the odds and many misunderstandings among us, I do feel grateful to them for helping me in my trying times. Supporting my staff is my way of paying back, by extending help to those who need it the most.

To date, my staff working at the Thane salon, which has now been extended and made into a large shop, continue to stay in this apartment. I have a caretaker to manage the place and cook for the boys.

In 2003, we moved into a high-rise called Marathon Cosmos in Mulund, closer to our two salons. The new three-bedroom apartment had a terrace facing the flat, like a courtyard. It was a place where Harinakshi enjoyed entertaining staff and relatives, celebrating festivals, holding religious gatherings and hosting moonlight dinners for friends. The terrace turned into a centre of activity and fun, bringing some joy to Harinakshi, who was undergoing treatment and chemotherapy. All of us hoped she would recover soon.

I enjoyed playing cricket on the terrace with my staff members on weekly holidays. The terrace was barricaded with a thin net covering so that the ball would bounce back even after a high hit. We would even play when it rained, get drenched and end the day with sumptuous meals. During the summers, my mother made use of the terrace to its maximum. She would dry grains, coconuts, chillies, ginger, turmeric and jackfruit, peel areca nuts, dry clothes, and take a stroll for some fresh air early in the day. I would exercise there in the mornings and use the place like a sit-out in the late evenings.

Our joy seemed to be snatched from us though, as Harinakshi's health worsened. To see her suffering was the most dreadful part of my life. Harinakshi's pain was like my own. I felt helpless and miserable as I did all I could to give her the best treatment. She passed away in the same house and our last exchange of words was also here—an unforgettable moment that gave no indication to me that her end was so close. Her body was laid in the house for the last rites and after that, the funeral followed.

Her demise created a huge vacuum in my life. I tried to

stay busy, working from the crack of dawn to late in the night. The revelry on the terrace seemed to belong to another lifetime. The place was stone dead. I hesitated to open the door to the terrace. It would remind me of how she used to wait there for me in the evening. There were times when I have walked in there and felt as though she were calling out my name. I would look around and barge into the terrace only to find an empty space. I would sense her presence everywhere in the house. Life had taken a somersault… once again.

As the months rolled by, my salon at Lokhandwala began attracting a huge number of clients, many from the glamour world. Travelling from Mulund to attend to a number of celebrity clients in Lokhandwala, and visiting three other salons apart from giving time to the teaching academy at Andheri Link Road, was turning out to be chaotic and hectic. I contemplated shifting to the western suburbs.

A friend took me to a newly constructed towering building at Oshiwara. That evening, as I walked into the ready apartment, I saw the flaming orange sky and the sun dipping gradually in the horizon. It was truly mesmerising. I fell in love with the place at that very moment. I stood in the huge balcony of the thirty-sixth floor for some time. As the sun set, I saw a swathe of tiny lights twinkling.

From up there, I could see the lights turned on in the homes below. It's a spectacle that has always fascinated me. For me, the sky sparkling in the farthest end of the visible horizon is an almost magical sight. It rekindles a feeling of newness and hope and adds a spring in my step. It reminds me of the day I left my hometown many years ago, when I watched the same magical sky light up on my way to Mumbai while travelling in the bus. It fills me with happiness.

I knew this was the place for me, my mother and my new family. Anushree had already come into my life and we had

had our first child, Rohil, while we were still in the Mulund apartment.

This house is plush, has more rooms and a large living area that fills up with the children's banter. My daughter Aaradhya was born after we shifted. My mother's room has a special enclosure for Goddess Kateel Durgaparmeshwari, the most revered deity for us and for people in our hometown. Children enjoy playing in the lawns below, swimming, and celebrating birthday parties in the community hall. During the monsoons, the air becomes foggy and every now and then, you can feel the clouds coming closer.

Fitted with large windows, the sky overlooks all rooms facing the western horizon. I like to see the stars twinkle when I come home to sleep late in the night. As I watch them shine, I feel like I want to reach out there.

I once had a small dream of owning a salon made out of coconut palms. All I needed was a chair, a pair of barber's scissors, a comb and a shaving blade with a small mirror. It was but a small wish. But God had other plans. Grand plans.

Today, it is work and only work. At the crack of dawn, I am at the club to play tennis or at the gymnasium for a workout. Then my schedule begins with travelling distances—it could be my salon either in South Mumbai or somewhere in the middle of the city or in the northern end, in Dombivali. Mostly, I have back-to-back appointments with clients, many of whom are loyal patrons of my salons, who specially ask for me to cut their hair.

Nowadays, I dedicate considerable time visiting the homes or offices of clients who are celebrities, corporate bigwigs and people known to be leaders in their field of work. Paucity of time prevents them from visiting my salon, and so I opt to personally be there at their place. It brings back memories of my young days, when I would visit the homes of wealthy landlords.

Despite all the luxury at my disposal, at heart, I am still the simple man who belongs to a remote village in the south of India. Even today, I can sleep or stay anywhere without feeling any discomfort. In Mumbai, there are some who have breakfast in a five-star hotel and dinner in a seven-star one. As for me, I prefer to carry along my box of homemade food. At the end of the day, my wish is to go back home and be with my family. My needs are few. In Mumbai's hot and humid weather, I am quite comfortable with a fan running at a slow speed, just about sufficient to keep the air fresh. When sleep overpowers me, I simply rest. Often, a folded towel under my head.

Every night, when I hit the bed, I watch the twinkling, bejewelled sky as my eyes close. And I am at peace.

If you want to walk fast, walk alone. But if you want to walk far, walk together.

—Ratan Tata, former chairman of Tata Sons and philanthropist

chapter eighteen

THE COMMUNITY STRIVES TO KEEP THE ANCESTRAL PROFESSION ALIVE

The name Bhandary is synonymous with being a barber in the Dakshina Kannada and Udupi districts, which includes cities, towns and villages around the port city of Mangalore. Local residents universally refer to the region as 'ooru', meaning their hometown or the place their ancestors belonged to, but geographically speaking, the native home could be located anywhere in the region.

A Bhandary's scissors move like no one else's—this is the local catchphrase in Tulu, Kannada and Konkani, languages spoken by the people residing in these areas. It is a popular belief that a Bhandary is sure to be successful like none other in the salon business.

In the book, it is noticeable that my second name, Bhandary, belongs to all my relatives from the maternal as well as the paternal side of the family, including friends from within the community. Since the surname is very common, identifying the different people mentioned in this book and understanding my relationship with them might appear confusing to readers and people unfamiliar with the region.

This line of work is typical to our lineage and dates back to the era of my forefathers. Senior members of the community say that it is not known exactly when the clan decided to take up the barber's profession. However, they recollect that people from the Bhandary community were exclusively called upon to offer their services to princely and affluent families.

Historically, kings were known to have court barbers who assumed the role of emissaries as well as confidantes. The nature of their work demanded physical proximity to the client and, as a result, they became close to the rulers. Over generations, the wealthy, upper-caste families patronised barbers, inviting them to their homes to do the job, while the common man visited the salon.

Being a barber was considered a lowly profession and was meant to be undertaken by the backward, economically underprivileged community. A few exceptions owned farmland and lived off its agricultural produce. Education, even attending school, was never considered a priority.

Today, this community of nearly sixty thousand people, a relatively small number, has more than half of its population residing in and around Mangalore. Others have, for better opportunities, migrated to cities like Mumbai and overseas, particularly to the Middle East.

Nowadays, I notice that the young generation is more focused on building a secure life; I see a keenness to pursue higher education and become professionally qualified in the fields of medicine, engineering, information technology, finance, law and media.

Earlier, the youth of our community lacked this focus. Sometimes they opted to work as waiters in hotels in Mumbai, despite the gruelling struggle it entailed. They shacked up with fellow mates from towns and villages, worked all day, and studied in night schools. The qualified ones were few, and they obviously took up well-paid or professional jobs.

Family-run haircutting salons were ordinary shops set up in

cramped places like street corners or by the pavement, with sparse furniture catering only to males. A barber's shop was by no means considered a lucrative business; the returns were too measly. Armed with a handful of tools such as a comb, scissors, a water spray, a rudimentary four-finger blade to work out a buzz effect on the nape, and a knife to shave, the barber's job was to snip hair, shave or trim beards and give head massages on demand.

But with time, old methods became defunct and modern gadgets ushered in better prospects. Swanky salons and top-end parlours began to proliferate. The beauty and hair care industry has turned into a viable business over the last two decades, giving much-needed respect and status to those running the trade.

The Bhandary Mahamandala Association (BMA), established in August 2011 with the aim of bringing all the people of the community together under one umbrella, has ushered in a wave of new change. With over two thousand members, it is making focused efforts to create a network by holding meetings with people of the community scattered in remote areas in Karnataka.

The association's president and founder member, Mr Suresh Bhandary, a well-known businessman in Mumbai, and Mr Somshekar Bhandary, a media personality who owns the Kannada tabloid *Savitha Margadarshi* in Bengaluru, took up leadership responsibilities. They travelled through towns and villages to mobilise smaller groups and collectively bring them under the BMA.

They continue to organise gatherings, address crowds and spread word about work-related options available to the poor and the uneducated. The youth are persuaded to take up salon work, more so if the family is already in the business, and are encouraged to utilise their skills and expertise by putting them to optimal use.

Young boys, in particular, are informed about the dangers

of getting addicted to alcohol and smoking. The bane of the community has been the availability of cheap home-brewed country liquor in villages, with many among the older generation having fallen prey to excessive drinking in the past.

The BMA provides guidance regarding advanced courses available in Singapore, Paris and the United Kingdom and information on procuring loans to set up a business. Many youngsters have started training under professionally managed stylists in top cosmetic companies overseas. With all this progress, the sense of low esteem and awkwardness traditionally associated with working in salons is slowly diminishing.

Women, who are mostly school dropouts, are encouraged to complete their schooling and further take up training courses in skilled or semi-skilled vocations. Others interested in higher education are supported with financial assistance or guided to help them explore their talents. With homemakers setting up salons in garages or small outlets in cities and towns, the business has become extremely viable for women making forays in the beauty industry. The possibilities are immense, with the availability of the latest beauty products, top-end hairstyles, spa treatments and new oriental therapies. Women can set up salons or offer home-to-home services after training in courses related to beauty care, skin, hair and spa services.

The BMA has also worked out a set of guidelines showcasing the processes involved in conducting the business, including aspects of training, setting up business, monetary angles (rates to be charged for the services provided), procurement of material, teaching etiquettes, retaining and maintaining of customer relations and adherence to hygiene.

With the help of all these measures, the community is more aware that today the business of haircutting is a major component of a booming service industry. They understand that the work itself is regarded as an artistic occupation which requires a creative bent of mind and that it has found new recognition. Other sections of society are venturing into the business in a big way, seeing endless opportunities for a profitable trade. Besides, the beauty and hair care industry has a close association with the glamour world of films, television and modelling. Then why should the barber community lag behind?

The Bhandary community's main place of worship is the Kachhuru Shree Nageshwara Temple, Barkur, in Udupi district, which has a history of over a thousand years. The Hindu god, Lord Shiva, Goddess Annapoorneshwari and the reigning deity, Nageshwara, or serpent god, are worshipped here. This holy place has now been rebuilt into a huge temple complex with podiums and halls to hold religious events, and it also has rest houses for devotees looking for accommodation.

In the temple premises, there is a huge sculpture of a five-hooded serpent in a separate shrine with a sacred grove known as Nagabana; it is the resting place of snakes. The traditional worship of serpents, chiefly of the cobra, has many references in Hindu scriptures and legends. To put it simply, the cultivation of land, mainly paddy, has been a longstanding source of livelihood. Snakes help in saving crops and harvest from insects and rodents and hence, they are revered and worshipped.

Over the ages, the community has had an active role in performing various rituals in the temple. In 1402 AD, a stone was laid indicating the performance of the auspicious Nagamandala ceremony in the temple by the community. The unique tradition of serpent worship prevalent in Dakshina Kannada and Udupi districts pertains to performing a night-long musical and colourful ritual to appease the deity for the welfare and prosperity of the community.

Thereafter, for nearly four centuries, the prestigious management positions at the temple were held by various groups at different points of time, including the Bhandary community. However, the maintenance of the temple and its property continued to deteriorate to such an extent that the existence of the temple almost became difficult to establish.

In 1988, the Bhandary community came together and began working tirelessly towards taking over the management of the temple, making its presence known among its people. In 1993, the community collected funds from its own people to perform the Brahma Kalasa Utsava (consecration of the temple idol), an event that was held with great zeal and gusto. Since then, the management of the temple and the organising of religious ceremonies and social activities have rested solely with the Bhandarys. As one of the active members, I have made a substantial contribution towards the temple's renovation and upkeep.

Mr Suresh Bhandary and Mr Somshekar Bhandary got the community together to organise the Nagamandala on 8 May 2013, the first in many, many years. Millions of devotees from various communities attended the rare event that provided meals to every person attending the ceremony. The mammoth ceremony was held on a grand scale, with donations and charitable contributions made by BMA members who planned the event methodically to make it a resounding success.

Earlier, in April 2012, the BMA held a daylong workshop on beauty and hair care called Keshavinyasa (adorning the hair) in Udupi, on an open ground, to create awareness in the community regarding salon work. Many of our community people, mainly those living in the interior parts, were under the impression that our profession merely involved giving haircuts and shaves. They were ignorant and unexposed to breakthroughs in the field and clueless about contemporary styles.

With a team of specialists from Shiva's salons, I demonstrated the latest styles on models and people chosen from the huge gathering. Crowds attentively heard us out as we explained a range of services provided in salons—manicure, pedicure, hairstyling, grooming for women and men, tattoo, mehendi designs on hands and feet, bridal dressing and spa therapy. We displayed innumerable beauty products and new gadgets used in hair and beauty treatments, which were available in the market. The workshop, aimed at attracting people back into the salon business, seemed to pay off as curious teenagers thronged to make enquiries.

Over the years, times have changed for salons. Not long ago, customers preferred to have their hair cut before 11 a.m. The men would bathe outside their homes before entering the household after their haircuts, and as for women—well, back then, women never cut their tresses. A barber's job was considered an untouchable's occupation and a visit to his shop required a thorough cleansing on returning to the house.

All barriers have been broken now. Hair can be cut at any time of the day or even late at night, depending on the convenience of clients, who have busy careers and fast-paced lives. Shiva's salons clearly believe in the dictum that 'customer is king'. Our salons are open until the last customer is attended to… to his or her satisfaction.

Confront the dark parts of yourself and work to banish them with illumination and forgiveness. Your willingness to wrestle with your demons will cause your angels to sing.

—*August Wilson, playwright, winner of the Pulitzer Prize*

chapter nineteen

Taste, Sight, Sound and Smell

Gurgling Streams

The familiar sound of water gushing down the stream lured me towards the rivulet barricaded with thorny bushes and magenta bougainvillea. There is a water-pumping station behind the now-closed salon in Durgadabetta, in Yelemadalu village, where I meet Kittu Anjara, a forty-nine-year-old tea estate worker, who was checking out pipes and the steady flow of water. I enquire about the salon, now locked and lying in a decrepit condition in the compound. He begins to reminisce about the place, about how as a young boy, he would visit the salon for a haircut. He recalls my uncle easily, but not me.

'There used to be a young boy named Shivarama working here,' I try to remind Anjara. He looks straight into my eyes for a moment, then blinks—a vacant, pensive look in his eyes. He seems lost in thought. 'What happened to him?' I prod a little.

'Yes, I do recollect,' he says. 'I heard that he had left for the big city, Bombay, to work.'

I get the sense that Anjara, just like the estate workers of old times who seldom spoke with strangers, is now beginning to feel comfortable with our conversation as I tap into his memories. He was a young boy then, he explains, his eyes gleaming as he remembers this bustling little corner. Labourers came here to unwind after a hard day's work; they shared family problems and village gossip while smoking beedis.

When I introduce myself as Shivarama, the same boy he had seen in his younger days, he stares at me for a while and then flashes a broad smile, revealing his crooked teeth. Giving me an affectionate look, he enquires about my family and then my work. He cannot hide his elation at seeing someone he knows from the past, even though I was only a teenager at the time. Then he checks out my attire—T-shirt and trousers—from top to bottom, and smiles again. To him, I have proved my mettle.

A similar feeling is voiced by Benna Gama, a carpenter who is now over sixty years of age, as he recollects the horrific shouts and noises that used to come out of the house every Tuesday, the weekly holiday for the salon. He too was quite young back then; he used to work in the tea estates when I was in my teens. I meet him in a small eatery opposite the house where I used to stay with Uncle. It is late afternoon and he has just finished lunch consisting of rice and fish. He tells me how admirable it is that I made an effort to walk out of the clutches of my uncle to make a life of my own, and pats my back.

Such admiration feels genuine. These are people uncorrupted by city life. There is a certain innocent quality to their remarks. They say what comes to their mind.

Both of them make me think of tea estate labourers, unkempt and dirty, trudging into our salon for a haircut. It was routine for them to cut their hair before heading for a bath, which used to be a weekly affair. They were poor people who worked all day, got drunk by sundown and slumped away in their huts.

Time has stood still for people like Anjara or, for that matter, even Benna. Back then, lack of education and limited economic opportunities were reasons that hindered one's progress, and it is so even now. Perhaps it has changed for many labourers and poor people who left these forest areas and estate work for greener pastures. Hence, anybody who steps out of the confines of this quaint village to pursue a new way of life evokes a sense of respect among those who have stayed behind.

Over the years, the picturesque Durgadabetta area remains enchantingly beautiful. Winter is almost winding up, summer is approaching, and yet, the weather is pleasant. All year long, the climate is wonderfully cool.

Nearly four decades ago, the bus travel from the main town, Karkala, to Yelemadalu used to be a day-long arduous journey, requiring changing of buses at different towns. From the warm climes of Karkala, we would travel by bus to Hebri, then take a different bus to the temple town of Someshwara, and wait for an hour to get into a tempo that would ascend the Agumbe hill section to the cold town of Koppa. From there, we would have to travel by bus to Jaipura and again alight to hitch a ride by auto, or take the same bus to Durgadabetta, which is the place where Uncle Govind resided and ran the salon.

If I were to express now what that feeling of a daylong journey was like in those times, I would say that it felt as though I were crossing many continents to reach the destination. Setting out at dawn, going from hot weather to the cold beyond, meandering through paths winding uphill that left my stomach roiling, waiting endlessly for connecting buses, eating from the little food packets that we could carry with us and jostling among crowds in buses. We were lucky if we found a place to sit at any point in the journey.

Today, in the car I cover the distance in just about three hours. The steep winding path of Agumbe hill no longer feels daunting, the way up the hill and forest area is picturesque and attracts visitors, mostly couples who come to enjoy the beauty of the sunrise or sunset. Several cars and motorbikes are parked on the narrow road, some people sitting atop the roadside ledge and some couples holding hands—all gazing into the horizon, soaking up nature's palette. The breathtaking Sahyadri mountain ranges of western India greet you in a splash of colour—brown, mauve, green, blue, violet and saffron—and the sky glows with a golden hue. Today, I am able to take in the scenic beauty with utter admiration. But as a young boy, when the scene may have been just as beautiful, if not more, it hardly mattered; there was neither the opportunity nor the leisurely mood to enjoy that beauty.

As we near the Durgadabetta habitation, acres and acres of tea gardens over valleys appear like an expansive carpet of lush greenery. High on top of the mountains, casuarina trees sway in the gentle breeze. At the foothills, a range of bougainvillea in their magenta hues lend a contrasting colour to the green tea leaves. Below them, at the wayside, a host of periwinkle in white and pink strike a distinct combination against the clear blue sky. The place is an artist's delight and a very famous picnic spot. A number of movie shoots continue to capture the scenic locale as an ideal backdrop for romantic songs.

The salon, where I worked during my teens and where I found my calling as a hairdresser, is located at the corner of a road's intersection. To be precise, it is opposite the local post office which still functions, but the salon is shut forever. As I get out of the car, I feel the silence everywhere. The stillness in the air is quite unnerving. As a young boy, I had seen the place crowded with people and vehicles.

Now there is barely any human activity visible. The salon is a decrepit asbestos structure today, dwarfed by a massive electric transformer in front that makes it look like a rundown garage. There are weeds growing in crevices, tin sheets rusting due to the vagaries of nature, and the front door bears a lock. A yellow-leafed wild shrub happily thrives at the doorway, as though it knows that nobody is around to disturb its existence.

Karma works in strange ways. Uncle ran the salon set up by my father on a leased plot, and now, the shutters are down permanently.

A padlock fastened to the iron gate and barbed wire fencing wards off trespassers, keeping them from entering the compound enclosed with areca plantations. A well with water reaching nearly to the top, a huge mango tree whose branches stretch out onto the roadside, and dried coconut branches scattered on the ground are the few reminders of the days gone by.

This yard was used by local children to play cricket with dried coconut branches that were used as makeshift bats and stumps in place of real ones. Once in a while, I used to join the boys in the game since cricket is one of my favourite sports. Sometimes, an estate officer would park his Royal Enfield Bullet close to the well and I would steal a few precious moments from my work just to stand there and admire the two-wheeler. Later, I chose to buy a motorcycle of the same make; I still own it and I have maintained it in excellent condition.

A post office, a quaint little provision store, a cattle shed, a primary health centre, where hardly any patients seem to visit now, and a row of tiny houses and shops lie desolate. The only area alive is an auto stand where drivers idly await passengers, while spending vacant hours listening to blaring film songs. Logs of wood dumped beside the curvy road a little ahead of the salon dry in the sun and an odd Mayflower tree has branches mushrooming out.

Passing vehicles add a little activity to an otherwise quiet place. The whirring sounds of speeding rubber wheels resonate until the vehicle moves a few kilometres away. Buses still stop here for passengers to alight. A few get off and walk away into the tea estates. Trucks loaded with people hiking rides from village to village drive past and you can see the vehicles gradually diminish in the distance as they trundle down the zigzag road. Ambulances speed to the nearest town; in the opposite direction, a biker rides up into the tea garden; cattle graze on thick foliage growing by the roadside.

Who could believe that this quaint little corner property used to be the hub of all activity at one time? As I sit on the parapet under the mango tree, the silence is deafening. My breath becomes audible and my heart beats like a faint drum pounding far away in the hills. I can feel fresh air gushing through my nose into my diaphragm, staying there momentarily before slowly being exhaled from my system. I continue to take deep breaths. My mind begins to play havoc with memories of my working days as a teenager and the accompanying pain and sorrow.

Mango leaves rustle in the gentle breeze, creating silhouette patterns on the sunny path. Even today, despite the serenity of the surroundings, my hair stands on end as I recall the horrific days I had spent here. Every unpleasant incident comes alive once again, as if it were happening in front of me. I know it happened long ago when I was barely eleven years old, but that is just how we associate places with good and bad experiences in our life. Even an astoundingly beautiful place has the capacity to evoke pain and sadness, given its gloomy links to the haunting past.

My first visit to Durgadabetta was during my school summer vacation, when Uncle used the room behind the salon to stay with his wife and three children. I was invited here to assist him in his work. I was only a child then. I may have committed a fault unknowingly, but I do not know if I deserved a punishment as nasty as having red chillies shoved into my nostrils and private parts by my aunt. It saddens me when I come here. Wounds, even though they may have healed with time, do not fade away. The scars remain. How do you erase those?

Nonetheless, I value this place because it is here that I had learnt the ropes. I am grateful that those years of working as an apprentice and progressing to become a trained barber paved my way into a profession that is so dear to me now. I am passionate about my work, a fact that gives me immense happiness and peace of mind after many, many years of struggle. And this gratitude I feel towards my origins is the reason I never hesitate to visit Yelemadalu when the occasion demands, be it a family event centred around celebrations and religious rituals or just a casual visit.

In the salon's backyard, I try to reach out to the niches between the wooden strips of the sloping roof, just to absorb the surroundings. I feel moist mud on my fingers. Here I would hide small amounts of pocket money to save for a rainy day, away from the prying eyes of Uncle. That he never knew of my little hidden treasure, and that years later, he was dumbfounded when I told him about my savings, still gives me a rush of delight. I was able to hoodwink him—that is the kind of thrilling victory the child in me still rejoices in.

Further down is a gurgling stream where I would bathe, wash clothes and play in the water, all alone. As soon as I was up in the morning, I would have to wash my mat because I would have invariably urinated in my sleep. I could never help myself in this matter. As long as I stayed under Uncle's tyrannical roof, my sleeping mat was most often wet. In the freezing clime, I would rush down to the ice-cold stream of water and hurry to wash up before Uncle could get a whiff of my act; otherwise he would whack me hard, rendering my rear a lump of black-and-blue sore flesh.

Another patch alongside the same stream was like my playground—it's closer to the place where Uncle had built a small house on a hillock a few kilometres away from the salon. The water course, locally called *kalla gundi* or a stone brook, flows over black stones and boulders to find its way into estates and forests. I found my solace here.

When I used to feel sad, which was most of the time, I found my retreat by this stream running opposite Uncle's place. Perched on one of the stones, I would talk to myself about the pain and torture I was undergoing because I had nobody else to talk to. Perhaps the deciduous forest on the other side and its tall trees and shrubs were mute companions. They would know about my agony. They would have silently heard my cries and felt my pain. A dip in the waters soothed my frayed nerves and, many a time, my bruised bones and backside after a cane thrashing.

When I visit Uncle's place, I make it a point to sit for a while beside these cool streams. They have a calming effect on me, akin to an antidote.

The house still stands as it was built, including the stone steps that had been manually laid out one upon the other by both of us—Uncle and nephew—right up to the hill. The garden abounds in rare flowers, including a collection of hibiscus and rose varieties, and coffee plants. The cowshed in the backyard is empty. Wooden stilts, which were fixed by me in order to tie cows and buffaloes, lie bare, and the place stands desolate.

Coffee beans and red chillies are spread to dry in the sun in the courtyard of the newly built house owned by Uncle's family. It is adjacent to the old one, now on lease. The new house was constructed after I had left their home as a teenager, and stands in the place where I had dug up trenches to plant coconut saplings and fruit trees.

In the living room, my uncle Govind Bhandary's photograph is safely encased in a glass showcase. I look at his picture and hope he is at peace now.

Neighbours still recollect the disturbing noises and commotion that used to take place on the days the salon was closed. Uncle would go on a furious rampage, fighting with his wife, screaming and shouting at all and sundry, and beating me with a cane. Aunt's wails and her threats to jump into the well in the backyard plantation were a topic of neighbourhood gossip.

Today, a new life has taken birth in the house—my cousin's child and my uncle's granddaughter. Thus, a new generation will follow, erasing the depressing past over time. Hope springs, wrapping the household in happiness.

Dream Home

In the midst of vast swathes of lush paddy fields is a tiny salubrious village, Daregudde, surrounded by hills and forests. The beautiful landscape lends a perfect backdrop for a spot that Harinakshi chose to build our dream home in, supervising every piece of brick and mortar that went into constructing the bungalow named 'Durga Nilaya'. With one hand clutching her aching tummy and the other directing workers on every little detail, she worked painstakingly for its completion despite her debilitating illness.

Today it has become my retreat, a place I come to relax in when I am completely exhausted and need a break. It now appears that Harinakshi worked so relentlessly to make a home for me in the region I hail from. Daregudde is closer to the main township of Karkala and still away from the villages where I spent my growing years. The place seemed apt as the village is Harinakshi's hometown, and the house is located close to her parents' house. After setting up business in Mumbai, we made plans to build a house in the area. I required an ideal place that would be suitably distant from my relatives. I wanted to be far away from prying eyes.

I visit the village when work or social obligations demand my presence. Most importantly, the visit gives me an opportunity to rejuvenate, catch up on sleep, indulge in ethnic food with fresh fish and drink beer to quench my parched throat. Earlier I would call up Harinakshi's aged parents, who were caretakers of the house, and inform them about my arrival. A sumptuous spread of Mangalorean cuisine would await me, including the local brown rice called *urpelanna,* fried fish—fresh catch from a nearby river—and vegetables plucked from the kitchen garden. Now her mother visits the home as Harinakshi's father passed away in 2016.

It is an hour's drive to Daregudde from Mangalore's tabletop airport at Bajpai town. The atmosphere is relatively calmer in comparison to Mumbai's cacophony and the torrent of travellers at the city airport. The ride is smooth as one ascends the zigzag roads from the hill to the plains, passing through verdant vegetation.

Many towns and villages are passed on the way, all of which look quite alike—a mix of modern structures and ancient Portuguese, Jain and British colonial architecture that coexist alongside one another. Long stretches of paddy fields, coconut groves, areca nut palms, cashew plantations, casuarinas and bamboo shoots mingle with a variety of wild and cultivated flowers. Colourful hibiscus and jasmine grow in abundance—both are obligatorily used as daily offerings in Hindu temples, which are far too many.

Decorative gateways with religious motifs at strategic points lead the way to village temples. The traditional environment effortlessly blends with contemporary edifices housing educational institutions and information technology parks. Far away on either side of the hills and plains, India's industrial giants manufacturing oil, gas, petrochemicals and fertilisers reflect the growing city of Mangalore and its promising future.

White and deep pink frangipani and periwinkle flowers bloom on coarse hill edges, ranawara trees glow with tiny yellow flowers, forming pretty canopies on either side of the road, while the cannonball that flowers in the monsoon grows on the compound walls of educational institutions that dot almost every village in the region. The sheer number of these institutions reflects high levels of literacy, nearly ninety-five percent in comparison to the national average of nearly sixty percent, in and around the Mangalore belt.

The girl child, in particular, is given the opportunity to study and encouraged to take up skilled jobs, a fact that was noticeable at the petrol pump near the turn from Belvai town leading to our home in Daregudde village. We stopped there to refuel the car; a young enterprising girl managing the place filled the tank. During my childhood, girls in the villages never even completed schooling.

The road ahead is a smooth tar pathway. The first time I took the path with Harinakshi in a hired vehicle, a muddy lane threw up a cloud of dust in the air. It kicked up a fuzzy storm-like atmosphere, forcing the car to slow down, as it trundled over stones and evaded boulders and thorny bushes.

It was a bumpy ride but it had its fun moments. We had just got married. We turned right and left as the car skirted obstructions on the way to finally reach a mud-thatched house, which looked like a poor man's abode. The house did not have an electricity connection. We were sweating profusely in the humid weather and sitting in near darkness with oil lamps lit around. I was mentally prepared for this eventuality since Harinakshi had briefed me about their situation.

Our bones were hurting from the wobbly ride. However, when I looked into her eyes and saw the smile lighting up her face on reaching her parents' home, it took away all the pain of our rough ride. Looking back, the experience of travelling on the tough terrain seems joyful.

Our married life was much like that uneven road, full of struggles, hurdles and pain owing to Harinakshi's illness. Yet, in those tragic moments, we kept walking through, finding delight, happiness and fun.

Durga Nilaya is a house meticulously designed by Harinakshi, who handpicked materials for curtains and upholstery, shopped for crockery, cutlery, furniture, and even the tiles in the bathroom. She would not rest, despite the doctor's warning, until she had checked out every detail, including flower saplings, roses, areca palms, pepper creepers, water connections, solar panels and the paint. Her mother often remembers her; and as tears well up in her eyes, she is inconsolable. Harinakshi's smiling photo on the wall in the living room welcomes every guest. Everything in the house is just as it was when she left us forever. I still feel her presence in the house.

At dawn, sunrays fall in the room where I sleep. This is how Harinakshi wanted to pay obeisance to the Sun God as she opened her eyes. As a routine, in the morning, I take a few strides in the adjoining terrace to breathe in fresh air. Her late father Appu Bhandary usually watered the tulsi plant near the front door while her mother Ratna Bhandary would prepare a concoction of herbs and fresh juice for me and breakfast for the family. Before that, she would have washed the local brown rice and placed it on the wood fire as it would take a long time to cook.

The household is abuzz with activity during my visits. The aroma of curry leaves and mustard tempering in coconut oil for the chutney waft through the kitchen. On another stove, dosas are being made for the kids, Harinakshi's nieces and nephews, to eat before they leave for school. They look forward to my arrival and I like to pamper them. The smell of homemade food is enough to work up my appetite. It isn't that the same variety is not cooked in our home in Mumbai, but having such meals in native surroundings gives me a great sense of comfort. It makes me feel rooted; it reinforces the fact that the place which I once felt did not belong to me is now embracing me with open arms.

At sunset, I allow myself a treat—drowning myself in beer or Scotch. I take this liberty strictly in this house because I am aware that I do not have to attend to customers. It is a rule I have set for myself. I try to abstain from alcohol as much as possible in Mumbai, my workplace. I would never like to smell of alcohol as I speak, while styling hair or shaving the beards of my customers. I respect the fact that they choose to loyally visit my salons and in return, I like to be as hospitable to them as I can. I feel my clients deserve the best from me.

It is noteworthy that every aspect of this region has a story connected with my life. The incidents are filled with pain, yet a strong bond has been created by those very occurrences. One cannot take away the negative experiences from the years gone by, nor can one run away if one wants to; the past comes back to haunt the mind. Instead, one can make peace with those very incidents and build a healthy relationship around them, so that those episodes serve as reminders to be able to look back with a smile for having conquered those obstacles.

Even now when I enjoy a sumptuous meal laid out on the table, especially with family, I am reminded of the days when my mother and I starved and there was no food to eat.

Pots and Pans

The sound of pots and pans in the kitchen of my uncle's house still rings in my head. As a child, I could never gather the courage to join the other children during meals at Kabettu house, where Mother and I stayed soon after my father passed away. I always hesitated. I would think that I needed to be told by the elders of the house to eat, and so I would wait until Mother got back from the stitching unit job.

My mother's stepbrother, who gave us shelter in his home after the death of my father, is no more. His photo prominently hangs on the wall of his house as the owner and eldest of the family. During my childhood, there were at least thirty people residing here, but now his daughter's nuclear family stays in the house. The massive property surrounding the rather modest house is divided among his children; some have built houses there while some have left the land barren. The now-desolate ground used to be a vast expanse of paddy fields, seasonal crops and fruits. It had a large shed for cows that provided milk for the family.

On this land, there were enactments of the ancient 'Bhoota Kola', a popular form of worship in the region that involves appeasing local deities and spirits. The nightlong ritual would take place in the open ground and the entire village would gather in the fields to watch the spectacle. One such performance was organised by me a few years ago, with almost all family members present, despite the fact that we had shared an acrimonious relationship in the past. Mother and I have toiled in these fields, planted saplings, watered trees, drawn water from the well, collected cow dung, made manure, swept and swabbed the house. It is sad to see that those trees are no longer alive and the soil looks utterly neglected. In earlier times, the entire family worked in the fields, except for elderly womenfolk who concentrated on taking care of the kitchen.

Down the road from the house is a temple with an adjoining lake, a tranquil area where I spent long hours when I felt like an unwanted child in the family. My favourite activity would be to throw pebbles sitting by the edge and watch the waters form spiral designs. The feeling rankled within me that the same people who were ostensibly my extended family, the people I belonged to, were so cruel. They treated me like an outcaste.

As a consequence, when people shower kindness on me, I am overwhelmed.

At my uncle Sanjeev Bhandary's house, the situation was no better. Having more people in the house was equated to having more hands to toil in the fields and the kitchen. Hiring people to work was an expensive ordeal—labourers had to be paid with sacks of rice and money, besides being fed breakfast and lunch. In such a scenario, my mother and I were like labourers available for free. After staying there for about four years, we were shown the door.

The palm tree in the compound under which we cooked for three days staying in the open is in a dried-up state now, as though tired of all the disputes and hostilities that unfolded over the years. Uncle Sanjeev, now old and feeble, tries to maintain good relations with us, which I suspect is only a facade.

He keeps himself occupied by working in the salon he owns, situated in front of his house. The shop remains unchanged even after the passing of several decades. As a boy, I tried to get my hair cut in this salon a couple of times, but the experiences I went through ensured I never set foot inside again. My hair would be pulled instead of being combed and my head would be pushed carelessly. The family would rebuff me, saying that only the privileged were lucky to get a haircut at a good salon like theirs. I would visit another salon—one meant for the poor—since it was rundown and they charged less for a haircut. Or I would snip my own hair.

Today, some barber salons in Karkala and some neighbouring villages have a nameplate saying 'Shiva's'. It could only be a coincidence because the name Shiva is that of a revered Hindu god. Nevertheless, it makes me happy.

Even Kariminabai no longer lives there since she sold the place to a relative. When we had a huge row with Uncle Sanjeev's family, she came and offered us her backyard to stay on lease and ordered us to help her with all kinds of errands. It included working in the cowshed, looking after cattle, milking them and distributing milk to people who stayed in town, walking to the bazaar to fetch newspapers, buy provisions, and water her fruit and flower plants, areca and coconut palms.

Kariminabai's fairly large compound is still in colourful blossom. There were fruit trees such as chikkoo, banana, papaya, and coconut, areca nut plantations in the backyard, vegetables, and flowers such as jasmine, red hibiscus, pink roses, a profusion of saffron marigolds, tulsi and coffee trees in the front garden. Currently, most of these fruits and flowers abound. Casuarina and acacia trees at the far end of the property were like the mysterious woodlands, home to many species of reptiles and snakes. Green-coloured vipers suspended from branches were a common sight. They could be poisonous, and I have lost count of the number of times we mistook these dangling creatures for plant creepers.

The thatched-roof rooms have been reconstructed with cement to make a solid structure. The well in the compound appears neglected with overgrown shrubs and wild plants. How can I forget the death-defying experience of stepping down to clean the bottom of a well full of marsh and mud? Even seasoned workers are terrified to step down.

The need to earn extra money to be able to pay our rent made us take up work at a construction site opposite Kariminabai's home, where a Brahmin family was building a bungalow. As a labourer, my mother carried loose sand in a container on her head while I lugged bricks on my back. When I pass this house now, it gives me immense pride to know that our hands had toiled to put up this massive house. It still stands there, and looks regal.

I recall that on the housewarming day of the bungalow, we were served a spicy and tangy preparation of tur dal, locally known as *togari byale*. In those days, I had to go to bed feeling hungry so often because of our financial situation that my taste buds had begun to wither. The togari byale rejuvenated my taste buds. The taste of lentils and the aroma of freshly pounded herbs used to prepare the gravy continue to linger on my palate to this day. Anushree cooks a similar dish made of tur dal, which I really relish.

As labourers, we used to eat food served on alocacia leaves instead of banana leaves, which was the privilege of the rich and upper caste. The large heart-shaped leaves of alocacia, grown as show plants in gardens, are also used for medicinal purposes. The disposable leaf is shredded into half for two people and a meal is spread over it.

The hope of getting a small snack used to be reason enough for me to carry out errands enthusiastically. Two elderly Catholic sisters who lived in a cottage would feed me fish or tasty vegetable delicacies for volunteering to get their cattle home. I would walk my way to school in the morning as their cows would saunter to a meadow to graze the entire day. On my way back, I would bring them home.

Hawking Vegetables

I share a strong bond with my cousin Sunder Bhandary, now a retired army man, since my birth had taken place in a house owned by him. His mother, my aunt, took up the duty of post-partum care of my mother. I also remember him as the person who gave me a fifty-paisa coin and asked me to spend it as I wished. I was so overjoyed that a family member had gifted me money—that was something completely new for me. Indeed, it was a kind gesture on his part, done without expecting anything in return.

At the time, I was about ten years old and wondered if it

was a good idea to head to Palimaru to work in a bicycle shop run by Sundar's brother-in-law Sesu Bhandary. Palimaru is a township that is about an hour's drive from Daregudde. The sheer craze for two-wheelers compelled me to readily take up the offer made by Sesu, the owner of a salon and the bicycle repair shop. I thought I could get to ride cycles for free, without hiring one or paying a penny.

Today, the shop located at the village traffic circle is vacant, with a few broken chairs and a wrecked bicycle parked inside. At the side is another shop that is locked up, but a board advertises salon services and the availability of a saxophonist to play at weddings. I would think that there is a huge demand for musicians and hair dressers in this village that has a predominantly Christian and Hindu population.

In the market area, I used to sell vegetables, which was one of Sesu's businesses. Mumbai's vegetable vendors squatting on pavements remind me of my early days of negotiating to sell gourds, pumpkins and jackfruit which were grown in Sesu's kitchen garden. I would sprinkle water on chillies to keep them looking fresh.

I may have stood several times in front of the Ramanjneya Cloth Shop located opposite the bicycle shop, admiring clothes displayed on hangers and clip pins. I wished I could shop there since I owned only two pairs of shorts and one shirt. Each year, a new pair was stitched during the Hindu New Year, Ugadi, as the old one, by the time, would be worn out.

Now I feel like smiling at my simple wants and needs. Nothing has changed here. The shop maintains its old world charm. Clothes are put out on hangers and clipped with pins as a cautionary measure, lest they fly out with the breeze.

How can I forget my walk covering an eighteen-kilometre stretch, to reach the house of uncle Govind Bhandary's in-laws at Belman? On a whim, he had told me that he would give me some money and asked me to be at the place called Nitte on the outskirts of Mangalore city. I was so naïve to have believed him.

I had walked on foot from my hometown Attur in Karkala to Nitte where my father's relatives stayed. There I was told he had left the place. He was travelling by bus and I was walking on the road, barefoot. So I resumed walking to Belman to his mother-in-law's place only to be told on reaching that Uncle had left already. That was the extent of my uncle's callousness. I had walked all day in the blistering sun and it was late in the night when I reached the destination. The family there felt sorry and gave me money to travel back by bus to Attur. I was also given some food and water.

After returning home, Uncle was shocked to learn that I had undertaken the arduous trek. Everyone in the family was taken aback at Uncle's devious prank. They wondered how I could have taken a miser's word seriously. I was indeed gullible.

Visiting the temple at Palimaru was another high point those days. It always brings back happy memories. I would cycle away to glory in the early hours of the morning to the tunes of religious songs played out in the temple. The priest tells me that now those songs are no longer played. The serene temple premises are just as they used to be, tranquil and quiet, except for a few commercial shops in the area.

Sister at Peace

One place that is immensely close to my heart is a fairly big house, now named 'Soumya'. It used to be an old, tiled-roof house made of red bricks and walls plastered with a mix of mud and dried grass—building materials which were economical and hence used by people belonging to the lower-income group. The floor of the house was layered with cow dung and the plot fenced with tree branches marked the compound border. The rich, in comparison, had palatial houses made of stone. The new owners, who bought this place from us when I set up my first salon and my mother shifted to be with me in Mumbai, renovated the structure. Now, it wears a modern look with its strong cemented exterior.

This patch of land used to be a little closer to the forest area; it used to look deserted with just a couple of similar houses nearby. We had booked this plot for a paltry amount—it included the money that neighbours in Mumbai had collected and handed over to my mother to tide over the rough times that were to follow after the death of my father. Soon after we returned to the village, this amount was kept aside with my uncle Sanjeev, who used it, much later, to buy this piece of land. My cousin Sunder Bhandary, who was working in the army, pitched in with ₹50 to the corpus amount and we added whatever we could, even though negligible, from our own savings.

The plot was an uneven, barren patch, home to a pack of wild stray dogs. These were government-owned areas sold to the poor, so they were located far away from the village limits. The area is now a full-fledged residential locality with numerous bungalows, although dogs still hound the place, some stray and some well-bred.

As I pass through the narrow road in my vehicle, a stray dog lolling on the roadside looks up, shakes its body, flaps its ears and begins to yap. Another dog in a kennel by the road wakes up from its slumber and barks when the vehicle moves ahead. Their howls get louder as one dog follows the other as if sending a coded message that aliens have come into their territory. A few dogs are prancing on the roads and snarling at passersby. Their growls reach far and wide as every dog in the vicinity and those wandering in the thick forest snarl and woof as if it is their job to echo sounds. It is interesting to see how animals have a natural synchronised tendency to react to dangers and unknown elements encroaching upon their territory. However, I am still cautious when I see dogs anywhere close to me.

A tarred road has replaced the earlier mud path but it is still narrow in width. At one end it is connected to the main road of Attur, a few kilometres away, where a government-run public distribution ration shop was located back in the day. Mother and I would walk the distance to buy rations of rice and kerosene oil for fuel. Later, we could procure some sugar too. We would walk back together, both being barefoot because we could neither afford to buy footwear nor spend on public transport. I was nine years old, yet I was quite comfortable lugging bags on my shoulder while returning home. For lentils, we would trudge a longer distance together, to visit a provision store.

The compound area of the Soumya property has coconut trees, planted many years ago at strategic points by my mother. The house was built here with basic masonry as we could not afford expensive building material. Mother recollects that her brother Sanjeev had supervised the construction and lent a helping hand by physically laying bricks and stones while putting up the house. Later, she had cultivated other fruits such as guavas, lemons and vegetables and flowers for her daily puja. The house was fairly self-contained. The well dug up at the time still provides water to the present owners. During the time when Mother stayed here, her day would be fully occupied at the stitching unit, and by late evening, on her return, she would draw water from this well for bathing, drinking, household chores, washing clothes and utensils and watering plants and trees in the garden. After a hard day's work, it was a back-breaking task.

The garden had to be tended with care to grow vegetables and coconut trees that would provide for daily meals. Fresh coconut kernels were ground into a thin paste to make chutney and curries; and rice was ground to make soft dough for making dosas with the help of a second-hand grinding stone that was chipped in places. Nevertheless, it served the purpose. Now there are electric grinding stones to make the dough and chutney. Some households use mixers.

We owned this place for ten years and, for a considerable period, Mother lived here alone, while I was working in Qatar. She had to face numerous hardships managing on her own, and added to that, people in the neighbourhood played mischief. They would set wild dogs in the compound and throw stones to destroy her vegetables, mutilate her fruits and damage the house. Such wanton acts put tremendous fear in her. For days she would lock herself up in the house and cry alone. This was the reason I decided against returning to Qatar; instead, I decided to start my own salon in Mumbai with my savings.

The decision changed my life forever.

I sometimes look back and wonder how my life would have been if I had gone back to Qatar and resumed work at the stadium's salon. There is no doubt that I would have excelled at my job, earned very well and enjoyed settling down in the Middle East with all the luxuries one could ask for in life. But then, the question was how long would it have taken me to bring my mother along to stay with me? There were no answers.

Mumbai became our home and the place encouraged me to start my business and make it bigger resulting in a chain of salons. In this city, I have evolved into an individual in my own right, found an identity as that of a coiffeur, gained a social standing and have been well appreciated as a creative person.

There is a feeling of tranquillity within me as I experience the tremendous love and encouragement I receive from my customers. They are the reason I have been able to bear all adversities with my chin up. My friends, the staff working at Shiva's and most of all my family are my pillars of support. Staying back in India has had other advantages. I feel more rooted to my culture and hence make regular visits to my hometown. It does instil a sense of security. It also helps that I am able to prove my mettle to all the relatives who thought wrong about me in my growing years. Now, they treat me with respect and talk of me as the person who has made the community proud; while the young generation shows adoration.

Setting up the first salon in Thane was indeed a small step, but a momentous turning point in my career. It changed and shaped my life in every respect. All I can say is that today I am a happy person. Eventually, we sold our house, Soumya, in the village. Yet, I like to visit this place whenever I go there. It gives me a peaceful feeling. My baby sister was buried here, at the far end of the land covered with trees, shrubs and wild flowers.